Cold Calling's for Jerks

By

Kent Berryman

authorHOUSE™

1663 LIBERTY DRIVE, SUITE 200
BLOOMINGTON, INDIANA 47403
(800) 839-8640
WWW.AUTHORHOUSE.COM

First published by AuthorHouse 11/03/05

ISBN: 1-4259-0049-6 (sc)

Library of Congress Control Number: 2005909749

Printed in the United States of America
Bloomington, Indiana

This book is printed on acid-free paper.

Table of Contents

Tells the story of how the author received the inspiration for the title of the book.

Discusses the myth of cold calling. The lesson answers why cold calling is a selling model that has been outdated since the end of World War II. This lesson also talks about why today's Fortune 500 companies are still using this antiquated selling method

Discusses how many salespeople never get the word out to potential customers about what they sell. The author also shares personal experiences of missed opportunities and how readers can avoid these mistakes.

Many associates sell products or services that they physically don't use. How can you know the advantages and disadvantages of your product if you don't know how it works?

Many companies spend thousands of dollars sending associates to trade shows. The problem is, very few good leads are ever generated from these expenses. This lesson helps the reader generate better leads from trade shows, which in turn will lead to more sales.

Many a good customer is lost because salespeople are too busy hunting new game. If you want to make quota, you've got to keep communicating with your base. They bought from you once; they'll probably buy from you again.

Many sales people miss fantastic opportunities for future sales, simply because a potential customer is using a competitor's product. This lesson shows how helping someone else's customer can become a windfall for you.

Direct mail pieces can generate leads. This lesson gives examples of what has and has not worked for the author. Plus, it gives an example of a letter the author used with tremendous success.

Always a controversial topic. The author shares his own experiences with networking groups. This lesson helps the reader decide if a networking group is right for their product or service.

An isolationist country will never win a war. The same is true for sales. This lesson discusses how the reader can form alliances and increase their influence and sales exponentially.

Increased profits come from diversifying your knowledge and your products. It also tells a real-life story of a salesperson who was thinking way out of the box and made a large amount of money.

Nothing helps bring in new customers like recommendations from old customers. This lesson talks about how salespeople can get their best customers to go to bat for them. (*This is also the transitional chapter that bridges the reader into Section 2.)*

Section 2   (Soft Selling)

This lesson deals with why people choose one brand of product over another if both products are essentially the same. Helps the associate sell themselves.

It's not always what the customer is saying, but what the customer is not saying that's important. This lesson shows the reader how to look for subtle clues to see what the customer really means or wants.

The reason a cavity hurts is because it exposes a nerve underneath the tooth enamel. Most sales associates never drill down far enough to see where the customer hurts. Consequently, they never get the information necessary to lock the customer into place. This lesson shows how salespeople can expose the customer's real problems, thus leading them to the associate's product or service.

In this lesson, the author helps the salesperson transition from a selling role into a consulting role. It isn't as hard as it seems. Consulting can levitate the associate above the competition.

The Story Behind the Title

I wish I could take credit for coming up with the title *Cold Calling's for Jerks,* but I cannot. Here's the story behind the title.

When I first started as a salesperson in the telecommunications industry, I had a mentor named "Guy." You will read about Guy throughout this book. Guy was the best sales associate in our organization in Kentucky. He was a super-achiever (a rank that was given to people in our sales organization who were at 150 percent of their quotas or above. In fact, Guy had one of the highest quotas in the state).

Guy's office was in his mother-in-law's basement. His desk was a bumper pool table. When I first started out at the "Fortune 50," I would meet him every day and he would show me the ropes. At our weekly sales meetings, our old boss would always talk about how we salespeople needed to get out and cold call. This didn't really make sense to me because I was with Guy almost daily and he never cold called. Let me stress the word "NEVER." I can say with all honesty that I never saw Guy pick up the phone book and begin to randomly call numbers. I never saw Guy drive around his territory looking for new buildings going up (called smokestacking). I never saw Guy pull into a shopping center and go door to door. And yet, not only was he still making his quota, but he was blowing it out of the water.

One day, he and I were sitting in his basement office at his bumper pool table desk and I asked him, "How are you able to sell so much equipment? I mean, you never do any type of cold calling and you're always selling."

Guy looked up from his computer screen and with a straight face said, "Cold calling's for jerks."

Suddenly, the tears welled up in my eyes and we both began to laugh hysterically. Finally, after what seemed like hours, he began to tell me of his mentor, the greatest salesman that he knew. Apparently, his mentor had passed that little nugget of advice on to him. Guy's mentor had told him that cold calling was a lot of effort for very little in return. He said that if a person wanted to be truly successful in the sales arena, then that person had to build relationships. That day changed the way I looked at sales forevermore.

Being new to the business, I was able to try different approaches. I can say that without a doubt, cold calling seemed like the hardest way to earn a living in the sales game. I've tried it hundreds of times. I know of only one sale that was generated by a cold call.

I've known several salespeople who were great at cold calling, but for some reason, they couldn't sell enough to keep their jobs.

If you're tired of working harder—and believe me, cold calling for a living is hard work—and are ready to work smarter, read on. I think you will be pleasantly surprised at how much more fun non-cold-call selling can really be.

One final note, for the few of you "elite" who are able to cold call successfully and sell, read on; you may be able to add some new skills to your arsenal, too.

Lesson 1

Cold Calling Is for Jerks

Actually, cold calling is for salespeople who like to work extremely hard for very little return. Think of the cold caller as someone who puts all their money in a savings account at the bank. At one percent interest, it's going to take an awfully long time to realize any return from that investment. Cold calling's the same way. You'll have to make thousands of calls and knock on literally hundreds of doors for very little (if any) return on your time and efforts.

Unknowing sales managers have perpetuated the cold calling myth for years. Any sales manager who has come up through the ranks knows that cold calling is a waste of time and effort. However, these same managers are afraid to tell upper management the truth, because that type of thinking would be considered blasphemous. The vicious cycle now continues as these unwitting pawns in the corporate game keep their sales forces unsuccessful by providing them with misinformation.

I'll give you an example. Take "Ned Doorknocker," for instance. Ned's only been at 55 percent of quota over the last three months.

Ned's starting to feel the pressure. Today, Ned has a meeting with his sales manager. Let's peek behind the closed door and see what's happening.

"Gee Ned, you're just not making your numbers." Ned begins to feel the pressure tighten up in his chest. Ned's eyes roll from his boss to the floor. He feels almost ashamed. His head is bowed in reverence.

"Let's have a look at your call sheets." Ned's breathing begins to become shallow and labored, as he slowly pulls his weekly call sheets out of his manila folder.

"Oh, I see the problem. You're not knocking on enough doors. You need to hit the street more. Ned, sales is a numbers game. Starting today, I want you to make at least fifteen cold calls per week. That's only three a day. Anyone should be able to make that many in a day. That should get those numbers of yours back in line."

The sound you are now hearing in the background is the fat lady warming up. Ned's toast. I hope they need a sacker down at the local grocery store, because Ned's sales career is coming to an end. It's a shame too. You see, it's not that Ned can't sell. His close ratio is about 33 percent  when he gets in front of the customer. Ned's problem is he doesn't know how to generate good leads.

One of the biggest problems facing salespeople today is generating good leads. Contrary to popular myth, a good lead is not a human being with a pulse. A good lead to me is defined by a customer's willingness, desire, and ability to purchase the goods and services I sell. For example, I sell telephone equipment. In my opinion, every business in every town needs my products. However, the reality is, many do not. You see, most businesses already have a telephone system. Some may only have one outside line and one telephone. Some may only buy a certain brand (obviously the brand I'm not selling). Just because it's a business, doesn't mean it wants, desires, or has the ability to purchase a telephone system from me. My goal is to find that business in need of my services and try to sell that customer.

I'll bet you're saying to yourself right now, "This guy just doesn't understand. My sales manager requires us to make so many cold calls per week." I've got news for you. As long as you're meeting your quota and bringing in dollars, your boss won't care how you do it. In fact, if you will apply the techniques outlined in this book, you'll never have to cold call or do the "hard sell" ever again.

I'm going to tell you a dirty little secret. I'll bet your sales manager already knows that cold calling is a waste of time. I'll also bet that if your sales manager ever worked in the trenches where you are now (Did you know some sales managers have never sold? We'll discuss that matter in a moment.), they probably didn't like cold calling. And if your sales manager was a successful salesperson, I can almost bet they never used cold calling to make their numbers.

You may be asking yourself, "So if my boss doesn't believe in cold calling, then why do they continue to make me do it?" Another excellent question. There are a couple of reasons and neither of them is as complicated as you may think.

First, I know you're not going to believe this, but there are some sales managers who don't know any better because they've never sold. To me, having a sales manager who has never sold is like taking some guy who works on the assembly line at a basketball factory and suddenly making him a head coach in the NBA. He may know that basketballs can bounce, but he won't know how to play the game. In essence, that's what sales is every day, a competitive game in which you try to win your customer's trust and confidence.

Here is a quick war story. When I was working in the corporate selling arena, we associates were sent to a training center on a very regular basis. The instructors at the training facility were supposed to be the cream of the crop in sales. The instructors would spend a couple of years at the school before they were reassigned back out into the real world. Their reassignments always included a substantial title and very substantial compensation. One of our instructors was a very nice person, and she seemed to be very knowledgeable. One day in class, we were between assignments and one of my classmates asked her what office she had originally come from. She had been a sales manager in a fairly big city. My classmate continued to drill down (you'll learn more about that later in the book) to find out about her sales techniques when she had been out in the field.

"Oh, I never was an account executive."

"So you never went out and sold for the company?"

"Well not exactly. I was brought over from the corporate side. When my account executives would go on vacation or something, I would personally handle their calls."

Are you beginning to see my point? The woman did not know what it was like to go out and bring in business. As you can imagine, she lost all credibility with the class because she had "never carried the bag." (I got that saying from my friend Cam.) What I'm trying to tell you is some sales managers require you to cold call because some just don't know any better. They've never sold, so they don't realize it is a very inefficient use of time and energy.

If you're fortunate to have a sales manager who has carried the bag, then the second reason you may be forced to cold call is because corporate makes your boss require it, plain and simple. You see, corporate America has no grasp of the difference between what the sales force does and what the assembly line worker does. Blue-collar workers are paid by the hour. Corporate makes the decision that there are eight hours in a working day for that person on the assembly line. That worker gets two breaks per day, plus lunch. They figure that same accounting algorithm will work for sales. They take some abstract numbers and figure if you go on one appointment today, you will have another seven hours to go knocking on doors. The reasoning behind this is, salespeople tend to receive substantially more compensation than the average time-clock-punching worker, so they don't want you cheating the shareholders out of their eight-hour workday. There are two problems with this line of thinking.

First, salespeople rarely work eight-hour days. While "Blue Collar Barbara" is punching out at 4:00 PM, your appointment may not be until 5:15 PM. Plus, no thought or consideration was given to how much time it takes to get a proposal together, or even how long it takes to physically drive to the appointment. In other words, your job is not a typical day that can begin and end at a certain time. By the way, if that's what you want, you need to join Barb on the assembly line, because sales may not be the career for you.

5

Second, corporate headquarters doesn't understand the sales process. To them, sales can be a lot like Santa Claus. You just hang out your stocking tonight and tomorrow it will be full of money. But it's our own fault. Good salespeople tend to make it look so easy. Management figures you're just picking up contracts all day. You might as well get out there and beat the bushes. Plus, if you're out there hitting the streets, they have an answer for that angry shareholder who just lost twenty-five cents a share on their stock because the CEO didn't make their projections.

"The sales force just isn't working hard enough. We have this great product that people are lining up on every street corner to buy, but that lazy sales force just doesn't do anything. No, Mrs. Shareholder, our missed projections have absolutely nothing to do with the fact that the new product we've been hyping came to market six months later than we anticipated."

Why does corporate still hold to the myth then that salespeople have to cold call? Like all myths and legends, there are some nuggets of truth in there somewhere; we just have to find them. Think back to a time before computers, television, and cellular phones. How did people communicate? Newspapers, radio, and word of mouth. What if you couldn't read? It's my theory that cold calling was the way to make a great living selling back before World War II. You see, most men went to work and most women stayed home and raised the children. A good, enterprising salesman could go knocking on every door in the neighborhood. When the woman answered, the salesman could then espouse the wonderful ways in which that new product he was selling could improve the housewife's life.

What happened during World War II? Men went off to fight the war and women came into the factory to build war machines. They left the house. After the war, women were used to being a part of the workforce. They liked getting out of the house and earning a living. Guess what, nobody was home when the salesman came a-knocking.

You see, I think cold calling began its slide into ineffectiveness after the war. It began to take more doors to make the same amount of money, because nobody was home. The sexual revolution of the 1960s should have put the wooden stake in the heart of cold calling. It's my belief that for all practical purposes, it did. So why do companies still require their sales associates to cold call? In a word, "change." Corporate America doesn't like to change. Corporate America cannot bear the thought of a salesperson not knocking on doors because (here comes some corporate profanity) "We've always done it that way." Again, they figure they're paying you to do something.

Are you frustrated yet? Don't be. Once you know your enemy, you can figure out how to defeat him. To me, the first enemy of selling to me is cold calling. The rest of section one in this book deals with how you can find customers. Or better yet, how customers can find you without ever cold calling again.

Once you find the customer, the battle is half over. If you want to make money, you have to sell the customer. Section two deals with the second enemy of the sales profession, the hard sell. Cold call selling tends to be hard and aggressive. Non-cold call selling appears to be soft and peaceful (although looks can be deceiving). This section will show you how you can use the soft sales approach to build relationships, sell more products, make more money, and have more fun.

If you're tired of working harder and are ready to work smarter, read on. You're going to be amazed at how simple getting good leads and then selling those customers can be. Remember, cold calling is for jerks.

Lesson 2

Go Ahead, Tell Them

How many people know what you sell? Think about that for a minute. Do your friends know? What about your family members, do they know? If everyone within your circle of influence doesn't know exactly what you do, you are (and let me stress *are*) missing out on potential sales opportunities. In today's hectic world, it's very easy to lose sight of the fact that a significant number of people you know on a very personal level have absolutely no idea about what you do or what you sell for a living.

When I first started my own company, I sold all types of telecommunications equipment including cellular telephone service. I'll bet that I had fifty potential customers tell me they would have bought their cellular telephone from me, but they didn't know that my business sold cellular service. In fact, many people within my circle of influence still thought I worked for the electric utility company. I hadn't worked there in years.

Did you know that people will go out of their way to send you business? People within your circle of influence want you to be successful, but they need to know what you do. Here are a couple of ways that you can get the word out about what you do.

Here is a technique for telling people what you do without having to spend a lot of money on advertising. Many organizations supply their staff with business cards. If yours does not, then by all means, go out and purchase them yourself. Now think about how many groups you're involved with—civic clubs, church organizations, little leagues, etc... These people will probably need to get in touch with you sometime about some meeting or group activity. The next time someone needs your number, give them your business card. Remember, all these contacts could someday be potential customers. If this sounds obvious to you, you are correct. However, you'd be astonished at how many professional salespeople forget to carry business cards with them. Keep some in your car. Put a stack of them in your coat pockets. Throw some in your golf bag. Business cards won't do you any good if you keep them in a box in your desk.

When you're handing out your business card to your associates at the civic club meeting, don't be a jerk. Don't say, "Hi, I'm Kent. What kind of telephones does your office have? Who buys that type of equipment for your organization? Can you help me set up a meeting with them?"

Instead of being hard and aggressive, try this: "If you need to reach me about the meeting, call me at this number," as you hand them your card. "This number is probably the quickest way to get to me because I check my messages several times a day."

That's it. You weren't overbearing. You didn't say your occupation. And yet, the person now knows what you do for a living.

Plus, you've left the subliminal message that you're a hard, diligent worker because you check your messages several times a day.

If you or your employer isn't crazy about you receiving personal calls at work, try this variation. Give out your business card like before, only this time, write your home telephone number on the *front* of it. If you write it on the back, you never allow the person to see your card and what you do. Always write your number on the front of the card. That way, every time they need to call you at home, they will still see exactly what you do.

Before I give this next technique, I think I need to give you a little background. I live in a small town in Kentucky. This technique seems to work extremely well with car dealerships, financial planners, insurance agents, beauty salons, and real estate agencies. Typically, the business will run an eighth to a quarter of a page ad in the local newspaper announcing the addition of some local person to their staff. There is always a decent picture of the person, along with the caption, "Stop by and see Brenda at our location on Main Street." To me, this is a great way to get the word out about what you do. Even if people don't know you personally, they may know some of your family or friends, again your circle of influence. If the type of selling you do is point of sale (customer can buy a product or service on the premise), people may be willing to drive over county lines to do business with you because you're from their hometown. Consider this a transference of trust.

11

Trust transference occurs when someone doesn't know you directly, but they do know someone in your circle of influence or have a common bond with you (like being from the same small town). They transfer the trust they have in their friend over to you. In fact, many experts on rape prevention say that date rape can occur because of trust transference. A woman will go out on a blind date that was set up by a friend. She really won't know anything about her date, but because her friend set it up, she thinks her date must be a nice guy. She trusts her friend, so she transfers that trust to her blind date.

If people know you and like you, they will go out of their way to send you business. But before they can send you any business, they need to know what you sell. Get the word out. It will be great for your bank account.

Lesson 3

Use Your Product

I haven't mentioned this before now, but this is my second dive into the cool, clear waters of the old selling pool. My first job after I graduated from Morehead State University (I had to plug the old alma mater, since I never send the alumni association any money) was selling ad insertion on cable television.

Ad insertion happens when you're watching a cable channel like ESPN. When it's time for a commercial break, the channel sends a beep or other type of signal to your local cable company. This tone activates an automated VCR (called a VTR in the business, but who really cares) which begins to play a commercial for a local business. After the two minutes of local commercials, another signal is sent and the national programming is picked back up.

I hated that job. The reason I hated that job was because I was still following the old belief that the only way I could make a living selling was to go out and beat the bushes cold calling. Even then, I had an utter disdain for cold calling. However, I was decent at it and I was good at selling the service. The key to that job was knowing what programs were on and knowing the type of audience (knowing the audience will be discussed in greater detail in Lesson 13) the programs had. One of the account executives in our organization didn't have cable. She didn't know what shows were airing. Needless to say, she didn't sell very much. How could she? She didn't know or use her product. Is it any wonder customers didn't buy from her? I can just imagine her sitting in front of the customer, telling them that their customers were watching *Larry King Live,* when in reality, they were watching the World Wrestling Federation.

What about you? Do you use the products or services you're trying to sell? If you don't, start. Nothing can teach the advantages and—heaven forbid your product has any—disadvantages like using it yourself.

Lesson 4

Slappin' Backs at the Old Trade Show

Do you work trade shows on a regular basis and never get any good leads? I totally understand. In fact, when I worked for the "Fortune 50," we worked the trade show circuit all the time. We had the big, professional display board. We usually put out a big, working telephone system, so potential customers could try out our products. The problem is, we rarely had customers stop by. Maybe your problem isn't the trade shows; maybe it's the way you're working them. Trade shows can be a huge investment in time and money. However, they can provide good leads, if you work them properly.

Rule number one. Don't bring the entire organization out to work the show. When you've got three or four people working your booth, potential customers will go out of their way to avoid you. The general public thinks that salespeople are nothing more than sharks to begin with.

People feel intimidated when they see an army of salespeople all dressed alike. Why do you think people frequent car dealerships after the lot has closed? People think that with all of you standing around, you'll make fun of them or make them feel stupid if they ask a question. So what do they do? They walk way across the aisle, never even making eye contact.

Another reason not to work your booth with the whole sales organization is because when you and your co-workers are there, it suddenly becomes a time to chitchat and tell war stories. Suddenly, no one's minding the booth. Everyone's sitting around laughing and joking with one another, and no one is paying attention to potential customers. The next time you go to a trade show, see it for yourself. Notice which booths are doing well and which are not. Watch as people zoom past the booths with lots of company people.

Rule number two. Never put your good spiffs (giveaway stuff like shirts, hats, special toys, etc.) out at the initial opening of the show. I made this mistake at a government trade show once. All the booth operators were sitting there in their booths at the time the exhibit hall was supposed to open, yet none of the attendees were in the room. I thought this was kind of funny, when suddenly I noticed a huge group of people down at the far end of the hallway. Hundreds of people were lining up, waiting to come in. It was so far away, I couldn't hear what was being said, but I did see a blue ribbon blocking the entrance. Suddenly, the flash of chrome against light told me the ribbon was being cut. A virtual sea of people made their way down the hallway. Hundreds of hands were snatching and grabbing at my table, taking everything in sight. Every spiff I had disappeared in less than two minutes. The worst part was, I wasn't able to talk to anyone, because they just wanted their freebies so they could run to the next booth. At that instant, I knew how a farmer feels when he sees the sky darken with a swarm of locusts. One minute you've got a cornfield, the next minute, all you have is dirt.

Here's a better plan. At the initial opening of the trade show, put out some those red-and-white mints. Keep all your giveaways under the table. After the initial onslaught, the people who want to talk to you will wander back by. If you feel good about your meeting, it's at that moment you give the potential customer a good spiff. This makes the potential customer feel special because they are getting something that every Tom, Dick, and Mary didn't get.

It's at this point that you may want to replace your mints with some chocolate, like Hershey Kisses®. Chocolate tends to keep people coming back by, while the mints usually don't.

Rule number three. Don't put too much stock in the names you get from the fishbowl. It's been my experience that fish-bowlers don't tend to be product buyers. However, the door prize fishbowl is kind of expected. The fishbowl is trade show protocol. So when in Rome, do as the Romans. I don't give away a real extravagant prize. When you get back to the office, look at the names and positions, pull out the decision-makers, and toss the rest. It's not that these people aren't nice, it's just that they probably don't have the authority to buy. Take the few business cards you have left, write a quick two- or three-sentence letter telling them how much you enjoyed meeting them and enclose your business card. It's at this point that you tell them that you'll be making a follow up phone call. Remember, keep the letter brief, the recipient will appreciate it and will remember how you didn't waste their time.

Rule number four. Don't shout at people as they walk by. Be friendly. Make eye contact. But don't act like you're the fat lady's carnival barker at the county fair. Although this is not as common as it used to be, you'd be surprised how many trade show workers try to tackle people and drag them kicking and screaming into their booth.

Rule number five. Get to know the other vendors. Did you know some of the best leads I have received from a trade show did not come from the attendees, but actually came from the other vendors? There are a couple of reasons for this. First, vendors are in the business of selling. Therefore, they tend to be on the lookout for products and services that can help them. Second, because vendors see each other during down times of the trade show, there can be more time to walk by and strike up conversations. Don't try to sell anything. Just be friendly and conversational. It not only makes the trade show more bearable, but it also helps you network with people who can become great allies and great customers.

Rule number six. Show up early and get your booth set up. Think about this for a moment. You've spent a considerable amount of money to make contacts and meet people, so how are you going to meet people if you're late and are busy setting up your booth? There is always a lot of down time at tradeshows and conferences. People can't sleep in a strange bed. They're bored. So they will be hanging out in the vendor area. Consider these prime opportunities to meet people. If you're late, you will miss out on golden opportunities for some one-on-one contact.

Trade shows can be fairly expensive. The entry fee can cost anywhere from $300.00 for a small show to well over $1,000.00 for bigger ones. To me, that's a huge amount of money, so I'm extremely choosy about which ones I decide to work. Plus, you'll probably need a hotel room. You'll have transportation and meal expenses. You'll also have to have spiffs and a door prize. Some trade shows even charge you for electricity and other expenses. Don't forget your salary. It's easy to spend a lot of money. So, how do you know which trade shows to work?

The most successful trade shows I have worked are ones that have been recommended to me by friends and customers. I do these because these people know who is going to be at the show, as well as what they are probably going to be looking for. Having customers or friends recommend shows also does something for me that is even more important: it gives me a built-in audience. For example, I worked a local government officials' trade show where I knew about five or six people who would be in attendance. My friends would stop by to talk a minute. Other attendees whom I did not know would come up to talk to my compadres. Inevitably, my contacts would introduce me. Suddenly, the established trust and good will that they had with my friends was transferred over to me (here's that trust transference thing again). It was fantastic. I wasn't a telephone salesman anymore; I was "Moon's" friend. In fact, of the three good leads I received from that show, I made a sale the very next week.

Besides recommended trade shows, there are other ways to find out about upcoming trade shows. Call the local Chamber of Commerce in your area and ask them if any groups are coming to town. Watch marquees and billboards that may be announcing upcoming events. Check out the local paper for trade show ads. Also, check the paper's calendar of events. It may take a little detective work, but with a little effort, you can find the right trade shows for you.

A word of caution: Unless you're working a trade show where you have product on site to sell, don't get discouraged. A successful trade show veteran (I know he's successful because I see his work on about every government job I do) told me not to consider trade shows as selling, consider them marketing.

"You want these people to get to know you and your company. Believe me, if you make a good impression, they will remember you."

I agree. I think trade shows are an excellent way to build relationships. Once you build a relationship, the selling part is easy.

Lesson 5

Work Your Base

How often do you call your old customers? Sometimes, in our desire to plow new ground, we forget about those people we have helped in the past. That's a shame too, because those are the people who have trusted us enough to buy the first time. When I worked for the Fortune 50, I was supposed to land new business for the company. We had a group of aftermarket specialists whose job was to call our base of customers. I didn't particularly like that idea for two reasons. First, I had the rapport with the customer because they had originally purchased from me. Second, aftermarket people have to churn and burn. They've got to call a large number of people a day. Basically, it's cold calling because they really don't know the customer. They may know the type of equipment the customer has, but they usually don't know the customer. If you have an organization that allows you to work your base, then read on. Remember, working your base can put more greenbacks in your pocket.

When I talk about working your base, I basically mean you need to keep in contact with your old customers. I don't mean calling them up on the telephone and saying, "Hey, do you need to buy some stuff today?"

Here's my modus operandi. After we have installed their equipment and everything is running well, I send the customer a quick "Thank you" note and some Ruth Hunt Cream Candy (sorry for the shameless product placement). I want to make my customer feel special and know that I genuinely appreciated the fact that they spent some of their hard-earned money with me.

Around the holidays, I'll send my customers a personalized Christmas card. I always write something to the customer and sign my name. Too many times, companies will spend tons of money on expensive cards and envelopes and then not take the time to write something personal. To me, that comes across kind of cold. I want the customer to get the warm fuzzies.

Usually, sometime during the year, I'll either call or if I'm in the area, I'll do the old drop-in (I will discuss the old drop-in, in greater detail in Section 2). There's no hidden agenda. I just stop by and say hello.

When you work your base of customers, you need to be keenly aware or what they like and don't like. Some customers really just want to buy your product and then they want to be left alone.

At the big Fortune 50, we had people who would call customers five or six times a year. I have personally talked to customers who have said, "Would you please have your company stop calling us? We're happy, now leave us alone."

Personally, I don't want anyone calling my customer but me. I know I would feel a little insulted if my sales rep was too busy to call me.

Did you know that it can cost anywhere from four to seven times as much money to get a new customer than it does to keep an old one? I know getting new customers is vital for any sales organization to grow. However, I think that it makes great sense to keep in touch with your existing customers. Remember, they spent their money with you before. They trust you. Keep up with them. Otherwise, they'll look for someone else who will sincerely appreciate their business.

Lesson 6

Help Someone Else's Customer

Now before you make a judgment about what I'm getting ready to say, I want you to keep an open mind as you read this lesson.

One of the hardest things to do is to help someone who didn't buy from you. Let me give you an example. I have a customer who owns a trucking company. About six years ago, he bought a competitor's phone system; he would have bought from me, but he did not know that's what I did. (I should have followed my own advice in lesson two and told him.) One day, we were talking and he said he was having telephone problems. In fact, one of his phones at one of his more important locations at the facility had gone bad. He asked me if I could fix it. I said I wasn't sure, but I'd see. So a technician and I went over to his place of business. We did some normal checking and located his problems. He had several. In addition to his bad phone, he had some major wiring issues. We discussed the problem and "Shane" told me to go ahead and fix them. I did a search and was able to find a replacement phone. My technician went out and fixed

24

his wiring issues. All in all, we did about $700.00 worth of work for him. That would be well and good, but the story doesn't end there.

Shane has since bought a new facility for his trucking company. The building already had a telephone system in it (not my brand, but a good one nonetheless). Guess who he hired to get his phone system and his service up and running for him? Right again, it was my company. It wasn't long before he wanted to upgrade his system and guess what? Yep, another nice sale. Are you beginning to see how this works?

I know it's hard to help people who haven't bought from you. You've got your own customers and they should get first precedence on your time. On the other hand, have you talked to people who have a competitor's product and still need help? This, my friend, is a prime opportunity to take someone else's customer and make them your own. Let's face it, if they were getting good service from their present vendor, they wouldn't be complaining to you about their problems. Don't use this opportunity to verbally blast your competition, use this opportunity to show the customer why dealing with you is far superior to someone else; let that be your dynamite on the competition.

I think it's time for a sidebar here. What is your response when you lose a customer during a very competitive situation? Here's what my mind says when I find out I've lost: "I can't believe this person is so stupid that they would buy from those losers (the competition). I can't wait until that piece of junk lays down on them. Then they'll be wishing they had my stuff. When they call me up crying for help, it'll be too late. Or, when they do call, I'll charge them twice the normal rate. They'll find out then what a terrible mistake they're making now." Just once, I wish that I was wealthy enough to say that to the customer's face. Actually, I don't. You see, in order to succeed in the sales arena, you can't burn bridges. The short-term satisfaction of that kind of behavior would certainly undermine one of my long-term goals, which is to make a lot of money. So I may think that in my mind, but here's what I say:

"Well, I appreciated the opportunity to bid. If something changes or if I can help in any way, please don't hesitate to give me call." With that, I never act disappointed. I always walk out of the office with an air of professionalism. You know that they won't be as happy with your competitor as they would with you, but hey, sometimes that happens. Maybe a couple of years down the road, when they aren't getting the service they were promised, they may call you. It's then that you can slip in and take what should have been yours to begin with. In sales, like in sports, it's not where you start, but where you finish that counts.

The key to becoming a great salesperson is to build a large base of customers. I've found that a great way to increase the size of my own customer base is to help my competitor's customers. I'm not saying do things for free or let your own base suffer. I am saying though that non-cold-call selling is done through the building of relationships. I can't think of a better way to build a relationship than by helping someone who needs your expertise.

Lesson 7

Dear John Letters

Let me clarify something before we begin this chapter. As you already know, I feel that cold calling is for jerks. If you physically go from door to door or if you pick up the telephone book and begin smiling and dialing, then I think you are wasting your time. However, one of the most successful things I have found in generating good potential leads from strangers is the direct mail piece. Now you're probably saying, "Hey, direct mail pieces should be considered cold calling because you don't necessarily know the person you are sending the letter to." You are correct, my friend, you don't know the person. However, I do not consider Dear John letters cold calling. I tend to think of them as more advertising and marketing. In fact, if you are new to the industry in which you are selling, then you will probably need to do some things in the early stages of your career to get your name out into the public. I have found that the Dear John letter allows me to do that. In fact, when I started into the telecommunications business, I did not have a network of customers, so I decided that rather than beating the bushes, I would try a more consultative approach, and that was to send out letters.

I like Dear John letters for a number of reasons. As I said before, they make me appear more like a consultant, as opposed to some hack off the street. Also, they allow me to get into the doors of

businesses that would normally be closed to me. Next, sending direct mail pieces can be done without a lot of time or effort. Cold calling, by its very nature, requires time and effort. You have to drive to the location, walk in unannounced, hopefully make it through the gatekeeper, and so on. As you can see, a lot of time is being used. Hopefully, using the different

techniques in this book will allow you to work smarter, not harder. Time is the one thing good sales associates value more than money because successful salespeople never have enough of it. They can't have; they are too busy taking care of customers. Plus, Dear John letters can be fairly inexpensive to do.

Dear John letters on average will generate about a 3 percent response rate. In case you're as bad in math as I am, for every hundred letters, you may get three responses. However, depending on the type of product or service you sell, if you sell one of those three responses (30 percent is usually an acceptable close ratio if you are expecting to make 100 percent of your quota), you should more than pay for the time and effort of your direct mail campaign. Plus, the more customers you have, the more opportunity you have of selling them more aftermarket.

The following letter works extremely well if you are new to a territory. In fact, this letter did a phenomenal job for me when I started at the Fortune 50. To set this up, I did not have an embedded base of customers who were helping me network at the time. Also, I was considered new market development, so once I sold something, we had an aftermarket associate who would take over the account after the initial installation was complete. In essence, I did not have a base of customers yet. As I said earlier, this letter was a fantastic direct mail piece. This introduction letter had a 15 percent response rate. In fact, I think it was higher than that, because it was still generating leads for me almost a year later. Plus, I don't think I sent out a hundred copies of this letter to begin with. Customers who knew they were going to be building new facilities or knew their current phone systems were out of date would squirrel this letter away in some file cabinet and then call me several months (in one customer's case, almost a year) later.

Dear Business Associate,

Are your customers able to get in touch with your business quickly and easily? Is your current phone system a profit-producing asset to your company? Are you losing valuable customer messages because they are put on scrap pieces of paper or post it notes?

In today's business climate, helping your customers get in touch with you is vital to your company's success. *In fact, it costs seven times as much to get a new customer as it does to keep an existing one.* Sterling Communications has the things that make communications work in business. Our solutions have helped businesses just like yours serve their customers more efficiently and professionally. Plus, we've helped their employees become more productive. This helps you make more money.

Let me introduce myself. My name is Kent Berryman. I am the Sterling Communications consultant for your area.

Sterling Communications has been helping customers just like you solve their communications problems.

If your current telephone system isn't serving your business as well as it should, give me a call. I will gladly come to your business and analyze your current situation *free* of charge.

Thanks for your time. Give me a call. I can help your staff become more productive and help your business make more money.

Sincerely,

Kent Berryman

See, that wasn't so bad. Please feel free to use this introduction letter. Tweak it. Massage it. It may even spark your own creativity to design an even better letter. If you're tired of cold calling, a Dear John letter may be just the way to get you through the "no soliciting" door.

Lesson 8

Networking Groups. How Good Are They?

I've tried to make this chapter as non-controversial as possible, however, I'm sure no matter how I address this topic, I'm going to upset someone. Since this is my book with my opinions, I'm going to express them. However, if you don't agree, don't get mad, instead write your own book and maybe I'll buy it. With that being said, let me answer the question, "Are networking groups good for business?" Maybe. How's that for a straight answer? Let's first examine what a networking group is, then we'll discuss if it could be a way for you to generate leads.

A networking group is an organization where salespeople meet on a regular basis (usually weekly) to exchange potential leads with one another. Each member represents one industry. For example, there should not be two real estate agents in the same group. There are national networking groups with local chapters, as well as regional and local groups. There is usually a yearly fee to join, in addition to monthly membership dues to pay for facilities and food. Networking groups usually have attendance policies, and if you miss too many meetings, you get kicked out.

Networking groups usually give members a chance to stand up every week and tell about what they do or tell about a particular type of customer they are looking for that week. This is usually a timed one- to two-minute speech. Depending on the amount of time for the meeting, one or two members get to get up and give a big presentation about their business or their products and services. This is usually a ten- to fifteen-minute presentation. To be accepted as a member, you must be invited by someone to join. You are usually allowed to attend one or two meetings before you must begin the process of becoming a member. Once your request to join has been made, the group usually votes on you. A majority of favorable votes will get you in. To find out about the types of networking groups and if there are any in you area, you can search the World Wide Web under the terms "business networking groups" or "business networking organizations."

Now that you know what a networking group is, let's figure out if joining one is right for you. Answer the following simple questions:

1. Can you attend every week? If you cannot, forget about joining. Networking groups survive because people give their good customers your name. If you are never there, you can bet that none of the other members will be handing out your business card. Networking groups require a lot of trust. The only way to build trust is to be there every week and get to know the other members. Also, there are usually a limited number of absences you can have in a year. Most of the time,

that number is three. If you can't go, don't waste the group's time or your money.

2. Will you be able to sniff out leads for other members of the group? Networking groups want people who give out leads. If you can't bring leads to the table, you're basically dead weight. In fact, it doesn't take long for members to see who's getting leads and who's giving them. You can also bet that if you're always getting and never giving, your *getting* days will be numbered. In fact, that's the reason why I left my networking group. It wasn't because of the number of leads I received, although I rarely received one, I left because I wasn't giving out many good leads.

3. Will you be able to give out good leads? To me, this is where most members have a disconnect with each other. For example, a good lead for a real estate agent in the group might be an associate who is looking to sell their house so they can move into a bigger one. A not-so-good lead would be the address and telephone number of someone in my neighborhood (not someone I know, of course) with a "For Sale by Owner" sign in their front yard. Usually a person with this "FSBO" (pronounced fizz-boe) sign in their yard does not see the value of having a real estate agent to begin with, so basically you're giving the person a cold call and we all know by now that cold calling is for jerks. However, the responsibility for receiving good leads from a networking group will also fall on your shoulders.

You've got to be very specific on exactly what you are looking for in a customer (lead). If you're vague in your interactions with the group, you can certainly bet that the leads you receive will not be great. As a sidebar, don't give out your customer's name without checking with the customer first. Remember, you don't want to jeopardize *your* relationship with *your* customer.

4. Will you call *all* the leads you are given, no matter how good or how bad they are, in a timely fashion? One of the things members will want to know is, did you get any business from the leads they give you? If you get a lead one week (no matter how good or how bad), you'd better be able to tell the person who gave you the lead if you sold anything or made an appointment or something. The kiss of death to your reputation will be, "I haven't had a chance to call them yet." You can be sure that the member who put themselves out to get you that lead won't be doing it again anytime soon.

Here are the businesses that tended to do well in my networking group.

Advertising specialties – Pens, coffee mugs, shirts, logo items.

Auto Repair – This is a boom because we humans are afraid we are going to get ripped off every time something has to do with an automobile. This guy received lots of leads.

Cellular Phones – Although sales tend to drop drastically after everyone in the group has your service.

Florists – Everybody needs a florist because we all know people who die.

Home Repair & Improvement – This is a boom industry because nobody knows anyone who does this kind of thing. In fact, this guy usually walked away with three to five hot leads every week. I spent over three grand with the fix-it guy myself.

Health & Beauty – Hey, people are ugly and need all the help they can get.

Insurance – Depends on the group, but our guy did pretty well.

Plumbers – Ever tried to get one? Enough said.

Wedding – People always know people who are getting married.

My experience with networking groups hasn't been the greatest. I think, though, that a large part of the problem was the product I sold. Telephone systems aren't products that tend to fly off the shelves. I rarely got leads from the group (either good or bad).

Before you decide to join a networking group, visit the group as many times as possible. See if the members' scope of clientele is similar to yours. When I left my networking group, an accountant left at about the same time. He wasn't getting any leads either, although he did get my business. He joined another group with more professional types like himself—lawyers, physicians, stockbrokers. Not only did the quantity of his leads go way up, but so did the quality.

One final note on networking groups. Although I never made a dime selling something to one of the leads I received, it was a great experience. The reason was, I found myself a handyman, an accountant and a lawyer. Those people have made my life so much easier. Plus, I've spent a lot less money than I would have if I'd just picked up the telephone book and started calling numbers. Although it wasn't right for my products and services, it may very well be right for yours.

Lesson 9

You Give Help, You Get Help

During my senior year in high school, I did not know what I wanted to do with my life. I didn't think college was for me. In fact, one of my best friends and I talked about going to plumbing school. We thought we could go to plumbing school, learn how to fix a few toilets, and then open up our own business. One night, my friend and I approached my dad with the idea. We sat down on the couch and gave him our sales pitch. My father listened very intently, never really saying a lot. After we had finished, he asked, "Who's going to hire a nineteen-year-old plumber?" Good question. We hadn't really thought about the marketing end of the equation, especially with prom coming up.

Instead of plumbing school, I ended up at Mid-America Christian University in Oklahoma City (another shameless plug for an old alma mater) in a general studies program playing basketball. Our coach had a great saying about playing defense: "When you give help, you get help." This was great for a slow, short, shooting guard like me who couldn't keep a dead man from scoring. What he meant was, if

I was playing defense and my man got past me, one of my teammates was supposed to slide over and pick my man up. In other words, give help. My job was to then get to his man and guard him. My teammate, in turn, got help. Remember that, because it's time for a history quiz.

What do you think would have happened to Europe if the United States had not entered World War II? If you remember any of your American history from high school (provided you weren't asleep and drooling on your book), then you know that a majority of Americans did not feel like the United States had any business getting in a war that was being waged on foreign soil. Most of the country wanted America to remain isolationist. Then what happened? "December 7, 1941, a date which will live in infamy." Pearl Harbor was bombed. Suddenly, the U.S. was ready to fight. If America had not entered the war, there's a high probability that the Nazis would have won the war. When our country joined the Allied Forces, we helped shift the tide for the Allies. The Allied Forces won. We won.

Selling is the same way. Just like a soldier, a good sales associate needs courage, determination, and strong character. However, just like a good soldier, a good associate also needs help. No country wants to ever fight a war by itself and neither should you. Yet every day, many a salesperson goes out to fight the war of trying to make a living without having allies. If you're tired of knocking on strangers' doors and calling random numbers in the phone book, you need to form some alliances.

Attach or align yourself with people whose products or services are "cousins" to yours. For example, I sell telephone systems to businesses. The cousins to telephones are computers, alarm companies, copiers, office furniture; you get the idea. The people I try to network with are the ones in these industries.

What do you sell? Campers? Align yourself with pickup truck salespeople, boat dealers, ATV dealers, etc. Create a ('90s buzzword coming) "synergy." Synergy basically means one plus one equals three. In other words, the sum of the group equals more than what each person brings individually to the table.

Stop reading for a moment and begin thinking of businesses with the same type of customer demographic you have. Form an alliance with these people. Physically networking with people in overlapping industries can keep you from knocking on doors. However, forming an alliance is only half the battle. You've got to prove your worth to the alliance.

Try to send your alliances business. If you give your allies business or good leads, they will know you're trustworthy and they will respect you; and they will give you good leads in return.

Forming alliances can help you grow your business as well as your career. However, in order for alliances to work, everyone involved must be willing to give help or generate business for the others. Just like in a networking group, if you're constantly receiving and never giving, the receiving will soon cease. I'm not saying that you should use people just so you can be more successful. But let's be realistic—you do want people to send business your way. Form an alliance with others and you too can win the sales war.

Lesson 10

Look for Other Pots of Gold

I left the corporate telecommunications world to start my own company. My company's numbers have been much better than I ever anticipated. My company sells business telephone systems, voice mail, and wiring. As you already know, when I started Sterling Communications, I decided to sell cellular telephone service. I did this because customers were constantly asking me if I knew anything about cellular. I did not. All I knew was at the end of the month, I usually received a very high bill.

Like many of you, it didn't take me long to figure out that I was missing out on another pot of gold. One Friday night after dinner, my wife and I went to a bookstore and I proceeded to spend about $50.00 on a mobile telecommunications book. I read a couple of chapters and thought that it could be a good fit for my new company's business model. From there, I surfed the old World Wide Web and went to all the major cellular carriers. This took about an hour. A few phone calls, a couple of credit checks, and "boom," I was an authorized agent for a couple of major carriers. Sure, it took some effort, but in the beginning stage of my business, it probably added an extra $300-$500 a month to my net income. Plus, it gave me other avenues into businesses besides their telephone switch.

Here's a true story about a friend of mine who owns an organization that sells computer hardware and peripherals. It's a huge company (he and his wife work there). Anyway, "Slammy" had a customer who bought computer stuff from him. A few years ago around the holiday season, this customer asked Slammy if he knew someone who sold country hams. It seems every year, this gentleman gave all his employees a ham for Christmas and his current ham vendor just wasn't doing a good job. This customer was frustrated.

Slammy, being the savvy salesman he was, began to ask some questions. "What kind of hams do you usually buy? How much do you pay for each? When do you give them out?" Before long, Slammy had found out that the customer felt like he was being overcharged for the amount of hog he was buying and the amount of service he was receiving. Then Slammy made a bold statement: "I can get them for you."

The customer was kind of surprised. However, he knew Slammy delivered on his promises for computer equipment, so he agreed. The rest is history. Slammy now gets the customer his hams every year. At the company's annual Christmas party, each employee comes up to get their Christmas bonus and there's old Slammy, giving them a ham. He said he gives out about 500 every year.

I'm not saying you need to start selling pork rinds, but I am suggesting that there are many products and services people need on an occasional basis. With a little effort and resolve, you can be the person who sells that product or service to them. Big corporations do it all the time. It's called, "Diversification." They are always looking for new revenue streams. Why shouldn't you? Hey, you're the one holding a customer's hand anyway. Be alert and listen for opportunity knocking. Many a good salesperson is able to increase their earnings because they have tried to help a customer with a problem. Look for another pot of gold. It may not be at the end of a rainbow; it may be right under your nose.

Lesson 11

Have Customers Working for You

How big is your current sales force? No, not your company's sales organization. I mean, how big is your personal sales force? How many people are out there selling for you? There's a reason why super-achieving salespeople don't knock on strangers' doors or pick up the telephone book and dial. It's because they have an unpaid, yet very effective, sales force working for them. My company has a gigantic sales force of one. That's right, I'm the whole enchilada. However, my customers send me leads. And the best thing about a customer lead is, it tends to have a much greater sales potential.

Last week, I sent out two proposals for telephone systems that were generated by my customers. One customer gave me a name and telephone number. My other customer had given my name to the potential customer, and they called me. How's that for service? Guess what else? They genuinely enjoyed doing it. So how can you get your customers to start working for you?

First and foremost, they had to have had a pleasant experience buying from you. If your customers don't enjoy buying from you, they will not send any of their associates to you. I know that seems rather obvious, but you would be amazed at how many salespeople don't know the kind of buying experience their own customers have had. I can't stress it enough, to generate dollars in a sales career requires repeat business. How many of your customers would buy from you again? If you can't answer that question with confidence, then you need to do a better follow-up after the sale. When I used to work for the "man" (the big Fortune 50 telecommunications company), they had a group that called customers after the sale and asked them about their experience. I thought this was a sound idea. However, the entire organization was so big that by the time we screwed up the customer's billing for about four months and called them twenty times, their experience wasn't very pleasant. In fact, we had customers tell us that their experience would have been much better if we would've just left them alone. I don't suggest you call them up and say, "How was your buying experience?" On the other hand, it may not be a bad idea to stop by a few weeks after the sale and just see how everything is going. One side note here, if they're having some problems, be sure to stick around and help them get the problem corrected. If you don't have time to help them right then, you will lose all kinds of credibility. Don't stop if you can't stay.

Second, in order to get your customers working for you, you will have to cultivate a more personal relationship with the customer. I can say this without any reservation: My best customers are also good friends. These are the people I stop by and visit, without any intention of selling them something. When I'm in the area, I just stop by and say hello. If you want the customer to send you leads, they need to know you beyond a professional level.

Get to know your customers on a more personal level. Find out about them. How many children do they have? Who's their favorite sports team? You can be certain of one thing, if you know a customer on a personal level, they will go out of their way to send you business. I'm sure you have customers whom you like, not because they buy a bunch of stuff (although it's better for your bank account if they do), but because you have a genuine friendship with them.

Third, always follow up any lead a customer gives you immediately. When customers send you leads, they are vouching for you. They're putting themselves on the line for you. They're saying, "Hey, this person's all right. I'd buy from them again." Have you ever needed the services of a specialized doctor? You've never needed this type of physician before, but a friend of yours has, so you call your friend for the doctor's name and number. What does your friend usually do? They usually say, "Doctor So and So is great. Let me give you their number. When you call, be sure to tell them that I sent you." Your friend wants you to mention their name because they received excellent treatment and they want the doctor to treat you the same way. It's the same thing with customers. If they give you a name, you can bet that your chances for success are pretty good. You can also bet that if you don't contact the lead promptly, you probably won't be getting any more leads from that customer.

I'll bet you're saying to yourself, "I understand how cold calling takes lots of time and effort with very little return. I also understand these strategies for generating soft leads. But how can I sell the non-cold-called lead after I generate it?"

That is an excellent question. Cold-call selling tends to be hard and aggressive. Non-cold-call selling *seems* to be soft and passive.

The important word in that last sentence was "seems." Let me explain it with this true story. I'm a pretty big guy. I'm about five feet, eleven inches tall. I weigh about 235 pounds. I'm also a third-degree black belt in kung fu. I went to a seminar one time that was taught by an eighty-year-old martial artist named Professor Wally Jay. Professor Jay was probably about five-feet-seven and weighed about 140 pounds soaking wet. Professor Jay created a martial art called Small Circle Jujitsu™. In a nutshell, small circle jujitsu uses the manipulation of the fingers and the hand to control the opponent. When the professor would demonstrate a technique on a volunteer, he would twist a finger and have the person spinning around trying to alleviate some of the pain. The more the person moved and jumped around, the more the professor would lock them up. Before long, the volunteer was on his back, Professor Jay still had his finger locked, and the person would be giving up. Professor Jay would demonstrate a technique and then you and your partner would practice that technique. The professor would then walk around to the different pairs of people and watch the students perform it. There was a particular technique I did not understand, so when the professor came by, I asked him to demonstrate it on me. He reached out to touch my hand. It like someone had laid a feather on it. The next thing I saw was the floor as my face went crashing down towards it. Suddenly, that same feathery touch felt like a vise. No matter what I tried to do to get out of the hold, Professor Jay would just spin and move ever so slightly and he was able to keep the painful pressure on my hand.

To look at Professor Jay outside on the street without his karate uniform on, you would think he's a frail old man. Looks can certainly be deceiving. It's the same thing with the soft sales approach. It seems meek and passive, but once you learn how to do it, it will not only increase sales, but it will make the experience more enjoyable for yourself, as well as your customers.

If you're tired of hard selling, read on. You will be pleasantly surprised how easy and lucrative soft sales can be.

Lesson 12

People Buy from People

I'll bet you've never heard that old cliché before. There's a problem with that statement, though. There are two important words missing. The statement should read, "People buy from people like themselves." Now, don't misunderstand me. I'm not telling you to become fake (there are enough people like that in the sales profession now), I am telling you though that customers make purchases from people whom they interpret to be like themselves.

As you already know, this book is based on my personal observations. One observation I began to notice in the early 1980s was that car lots began hiring women sales associates. Why do you think they did this? Was it because women made the place seem a little more bright and cheery? Of course not. It was because car dealers wanted to make more money. Car dealerships knew that women were making more buying decisions about the cars they wanted to drive. Since women were getting married later in life, there wasn't necessarily a man in the picture to help the "little lady" go down and buy a new car. Some women felt intimidated by male car salesmen. By adding female associates, the car dealer was saying, "Hey, ladies, come on in to my dealership. You've heard of low pressure, we're no pressure. In fact, you can deal with one of our female associates." And it worked. Most car dealerships, especially the new car ones, have several associates there who are women.

I cannot stress it enough. Selling is building relationships. Think about the people you hang around with. The people you go to church with. The people who live in your neighborhood. I would bet that most of the people in your social circles are people who have many of the same characteristics that you have. We are comfortable around people who are like us.

So what can you do to be more like the customer? If the customer tends to be of a quiet nature, you be of a quiet nature. If the customer is a back-slapper, you be a back-slapper. Mirror the customer. Let them see themselves when they see you. Again, I'm not saying be fake and not be yourself. However, I am telling you to be observant. Relate to customer on their level. Remember, people buy from people like themselves.

Lesson 13

Read the Customer

As I said before, people buy from people like themselves. This is especially true if it's a competitive situation. By the same token, if the customer trusts and likes you (you've got to have both), then most of the situations you get into will never be competitive, because the customer wouldn't think of calling anyone else after talking to you. However, if you've been in this career for any length of time, you already know that there a bunch of good salespeople out there in the world. So how do you raise your game above the competition?

First and foremost, always know your audience. How many times have you misread your customer? Contemplate that for a moment. Steve Martin, the comedian, does a great monologue about knowing your audience on his *Let's Get Small* album. Sometime when you're down at your local library, see if they have a copy. For all you Generation Xers, an album was the way we old geezers listened to music before the MP3 player came along. Anyway, the monologue goes something like this:

"I heard there's a big plumbers' convention in town and a lot of you came down to the show. I worked up a joke for you guys. You members of the audience who aren't plumbers probably won't get this, but bear with me while I do this joke especially for the plumbers."

Steve Martin proceeds to tell this long, complicated joke about a "Langstrom seven-inch gangly wrench with a Findley socket." It goes on and on and finishes with the punchline, "It says sprocket, not socket."

Obviously, nobody laughs at the joke. As the album plays through in silence, I can just imagine Steve Martin with his gray hair and his white suit, standing up there at the microphone with an embarrassed look upon his face. Suddenly, he asks, "Were those plumbers supposed to be at this show?" The audience howls with laughter at the real punchline. This joke illustrates a valuable point. Always know your audience.

Here's an example that is more personal to me. As I've said before, I live in east central Kentucky. I never go to see an appointment in a suit and tie. That's not the type of customer I serve. If I showed up dressed like a banker, I'd be behind the eight ball from the start. The people I see wouldn't trust me, because most of them don't wear suits and ties. Knowing your audience is paramount if you want to make that good first impression.

Is the customer a back-slapper or the strong, silent type? As you have probably guessed by now, I'm not very shy. In fact, I was so confident in my abilities that I had the nerve to write a book about selling and then had the audacity to believe someone like you would buy it. I like to talk loud, slap backs and kiss babies. Some of my technicians accuse me of being a political type. However, I'm keenly observant of the customer's style. If the customer tends to be the quiet type, you can bet that my style changes very quickly and very subtly. According to some research, a customer will make a decision about whether they will buy from you after about thirty seconds.

This point was hammered home to me at a sales training course in Denver. The class did a mock training exercise where one of us would pretend to be meeting a customer on their premises. The instructor played the part of the customer, and everyone sat and watched as the salesperson explained about a piece of telephone equipment. We had a woman in the group who was a real touchy-feely type. As the role play begins, she goes to the customer's site and introduces herself. As my classmate begins explaining about the product, she starts touching the customer's shoulder. The instructor continues to move away from her, but like a magnet, she pulls back up beside him and is touching him again. After her exercise, the instructor says, "Keep your hands off me. Couldn't you tell by the way I was moving away from you that you were making me uncomfortable?" She didn't even realize. She was just being herself. I'm not trying to tell you to be someone you're not. On the other hand, you need to be able to read your customer enough to know when they are uncomfortable with something in your actions or personality.

Mirror the customer. Mirroring is a technique in which you position yourself exactly as the customer is. If they're leaning forward with their hands crossed in their lap, then you try leaning forward toward them with you hands crossed in your lap. If they're leaning back with their fingers locked behind their head, then you try leaning back with you fingers locked behind you head. Mirroring can help create a subliminal common bond between you and the customer.

What is the customer audibly saying? Don't just hear them, but genuinely listen to them.

Here's a little observational quiz. How would you handle the following situation? You arrive for your 1:30 appointment with the customer. You start off with some happy talk like, "So Joan, how's it been going today?"

"Not too good. We've had all kinds of problems in the plant today. In fact, I just got back to my office about five minutes before you showed up. I haven't even had a chance to eat lunch yet."

What would you do next?

a. Console the customer.
b. Ask the customer if this is a bad time and would they like to reschedule the appointment.
c. Pretend you didn't hear them and start your fact find.
d. Tell them this won't take too long.

In my opinion, the correct answer is "b." Here's why. The customer has just told you she's been having problems all day. Even if everything is now fixed (and there's a good chance it isn't) her mind won't be with you. More than likely, she won't give you all the information she needs to, so you will probably be submitting several updated proposals, because as she remembers things later on, she'll be calling you with things she forgot in her harried state of mind. In other words, more work for you. Or she may not tell you everything, but the competition's appointment may be tomorrow and they will more than likely get some key information that you did not get today. The competition will have a better grasp of the problem than you will.

Next, she's hungry. Have you ever tried to concentrate on an empty stomach? It's impossible. Why do you think the people at your church start getting a little restless about noon? It's because we humans have been conditioned to eat at midday. When we miss that meal, we've suddenly been thrown off schedule, both physically and mentally.

I think you should ask the customer if they would prefer to reschedule and let them decide. This does a couple of things. It lets the customer know that you are concerned about their time (not to mention your own). It also shows the customer you are considerate. You can bet they will give you every benefit of the doubt when you come back to see them.

Always listen for audible clues when reading the customer. Notice the pacing. The types of descriptions the customer is using. Remember you are looking for every advantage.

Next, what is the customer visually saying? There are all kinds of books written on the subject of body language and what it can tell us. I think we all know what the raised middle finger means, that's pretty obvious. I'm talking about the other reflexive gestures like crossed arms, fingers tapping on the desk, the rattling of coins in a pocket, the scratching of the nose, and other non-verbal cues.

Crossed arms may be telling you that the customer is closed to what you are saying. Fingers tapping on the desk could signify "You're boring me." The rattling of coins can mean "Time is money and my time is valuable." The scratching of the nose can mean the customer may not be telling you the whole truth. A word of caution here: Body language needs to be studied in the entire context of the situation. In other words, the customer may be lying when they scratch their nose or they may just have an itch.

Reading the customer isn't a difficult skill to hone. Customers will give out all kinds of clues both visually and audibly; you've just got to pay attention. Soft selling requires that you not only know your customer, but you also have to be able to read between the lines of what they are really saying and how they are really saying it.

Lesson 14

Drilling for Oil

Actually, I probably should have called this chapter "Drilling for Gold" because our goal is to get the customer's "gold" or money and make it our own; but you don't drill for gold, you dig for it. However, I need your mind to think of how people drill for oil, because you need to be a good "Roughneck" (someone who drills for oil) if you want to be a good salesperson. Confused yet? Don't worry about it. By the end of this chapter, you will know exactly what I'm talking about.

Here's a little role play scenario to help get the point across. Let's look at a couple of window salespeople as they go and see "Todd, the Troubled Customer." Todd is building a brand new facility because his auto repair business has grown significantly over the last couple of years. In fact, Todd feels like his business will experience double-digit growth for another three years before it finally begins to level off. Todd's old shop was a garage that was built in the 1950s. It had a dark, cramped waiting room. In fact, Todd feels like he has lost customers because there was no place for them to sit. He believes in the pack mentality. Todd envisions a showplace waiting area that is well-lit and roomy. He feels like he can get more customers if they drive by his new location and see his big waiting room full of people. In other words, people want to belong to a group, and if they see others at his place, then they will want to come to his place, too. Todd wants energy efficiency as well. Todd has calculated that his old, drafty shop cost him an extra $12,000.00 a year in wasted energy expenses. Todd is not cheap. However, like most building projects, this one is 10 percent over budget. Todd doesn't know a lot about windows and doors. Let's meet our first associate, "Slick-Talking Steve."

Steve pulls onto the construction site. As he gets out of his car, he's already begun to count the number of window spaces he sees. After finding out which person on site is Todd, Steve heads over to talk with his prospective customer. A few pleasantries later, Steve begins his fact-find.

"So, Todd, how many windows are you going to need?"

"We'll have ten normal-type, in addition to the three large ones I want for the waiting room."

"What about glass doors?"

"I want one glass door for the customer entrance and I haven't really decided about the garage doors."

"Yea, garage doors can be tricky." Steve's mind begins to add up all the commission he could make. The sale would be decent with just the windows, but now that Todd has thrown in an extra caveat with the doors, this sale has suddenly become very lucrative. Steve knows he must convince Todd to put all glass doors in the repair area. "You probably want to consider our thermal insulated triple-pane windows for all the normal places," Steve says as he whips out his catalogue. "Here's what they look like. As far as the waiting area is concerned, you could go with the single- or double-paned glass there. You'll find those on pages 278 and 279. They're a great window, but they can be kind of pricey."

Todd begins to thumb through the catalogue. In fact, he does like the looks of Steve's products. "Those windows look nice. I really like those."

"Great." Steve hopes he hasn't lost his poker face. Todd seems to giving all the buying signals. He likes the product and he thinks it will work for his business. Steve continues, "Now we have a great glass garage door. It's pretty efficient and would really make the bay area look nice. What do you think?" Steve pulls out his garage door brochure. This is going to be even easier than he thought.

"Sounds pretty good. How much will it cost?"

"What's your budget?"

Todd's eyebrows flatten as his lips begin to close tight. He thinks that if he tells Steve how much he budgeted for windows, he won't get a good deal. Todd decides to play a little coy. "I really don't have a budget for the windows. I've grouped those together with the whole building project. Why don't you just get me a price, I'll talk to my accountant and we'll go from there."

"Fine." *Customers never give you any type of budgetary numbers,* Steve thinks to himself. *I guess I'll add this thing up and see what happens.* Steve pulls out his calculator and begins to punch in numbers, although it's not really necessary because Steve knows the price of everything he sells. He could never use his calculator and still be within five bucks of the cost; he just does the calculator bit to look busy in front of the customer. "Well Todd, it looks like it will be about $23,000.00 plus installation and tax. However, if you'll sign today, I'll take three grand off and we'll get it to $20,000.00."

Todd tries to keep his face as emotionless as he can. That price is about what he budgeted. On the other hand, Steve has dropped his price thirteen percent without saying a word, so he figures he can get a deeper discount when he starts negotiating. He does feel a little pressure, though. He really isn't ready to sign anything today and he still has another appointment with another window salesperson. He decides to put Steve on hold until after his other appointment. Todd figures that he'll still be able to get the discounted price next week.

"Steve, I've got another window person coming this afternoon. Once I hear what they recommend, I'll make my decision. Can I keep the brochures?"

Ouch. Todd just threw one high and inside. Steve was ready to hit the home run ball. He certainly didn't expect the curve. He decides to turn up the heat and see if he can't get Todd to sign. "Listen, Todd, I know you're getting close to grand opening date. I can't promise that if we wait another week, I'll be able to deliver the windows on time. What would it take for us to do business today? What about if I get you the installation at 10 percent off? Could we sign a contract today?"

"Steve, that offer sounds great, but I've already made the appointment. As soon as I talk to the other rep, I'll sit down and make an apples-to-apples comparison, okay?"

Steve tries to hide his disappointment. "Well Todd, that's fine. After your meeting today, when you sit down and compare apples to apples, give me a call. I'm sure we can do business." With that, they shake hands and Steve heads for his car. Todd goes back to the construction trailer. He'll find out this afternoon if Steve had such a good deal after all. His next appointment, "Dan, the Drill Down Man" will be on site at three o'clock.

It's now three o'clock. Todd's next appointment, Dan, just arrived at the construction site. Dan walks up to the construction trailer, where he and Todd shake hands. After a moment of "happy talk," Dan begins his fact find. "So, Todd, I see you're in the auto repair business. What type of auto repairs do you do?"

"We started out doing just normal stuff, oil changes and tire rotations, but a couple of years ago, I read about a garage that offered to check out used cars for potential customers before they bought them. I thought it was a fantastic idea, so I decided to give it a try. It has been a boon for our business. The first year we tried it, it alone grew our overall business 12 percent. Last year, it grew our business over 20 percent. That's why I'm spending all this money building a new place. We had to."

"Do you think your business will continue to grow like that?"

"Yes I do. In fact, our track record is so good with the auto check business that once customers know we also repair cars, they will bring their vehicles back to us for service. When you go by our old shop now, the waiting room is so crowded, there's no place for customers to sit. That's why I need the waiting room at this place to be so big. I want plenty of room for customers to be comfortable. I want big windows, so people who drive by will see all the activity. I want them to say, 'That place must be great at fixing cars; there are always customers in there."

Dan is using a great approach with Todd. He asked about his business. Small business owners and entrepreneurs love to talk about all they have accomplished. Who can blame them? Don't we people in sales love to tell our peers how well we are doing? Everyone likes to talk about themselves, and when customers start talking, they are just giving you ways to make your proposal stronger than your competition's.

"On the big waiting room, how many windows do you need?"

"Our original plans called for three."

"Have your plans changed?"

"I'm not sure. I'm a little worried about all the sun that will be coming in during the day. I'm afraid with big windows, the waiting room will get like an oven. Our energy bills are astronomical now. I'm afraid it will cost me too much money to cool that place in the summer. What do you recommend?"

"Well, we've got a couple of options. We could put in the three big windows like your plans called for. They could be double-paned with argon gas so they will be well-insulated. Plus, to keep all that radiant heat from the sun out, we could have them coated with a special tint that helps keep the room from becoming an oven. It obviously costs more, but it can reduce summer energy bills by 35 percent.

"Won't that tinting make it really dark, though?"

"Not at all. When compared to untinted glass, the tinted window looks slightly darker. However, people will still be able to see inside your waiting room, and that's the whole purpose of the big windows, isn't it?"

"Yes, it's very important to me, but so is the cost."

"I understand completely, Todd. Did you know that I've never walked onto a customer's site and they just handed me a blank check? The way I usually conduct a fact-find is to try to get the person to tell me exactly what they want, as if money was no object. I'll make a proposal based on what you want. It's at that point we'll evaluate everything and add where we need to add, and trim where we need to trim."

I will end the example now because my point has been made. Do you see the difference in the two approaches? Steve showed up counting windows. Dan showed up solving problems. Steve started out asking about the number of windows. Dan started out asking about the business. From there, he listened to Todd talk about his business. Then Dan found out *why* his business was growing. That led to what his future goals were for both his business and his new location.

So what's Dan's secret? First, he asked open-ended questions. You would be surprised at how difficult this is for salespeople, and not just new salespeople, I might add. It can also happen to veterans like Steve. When you've been in front of hundreds of customers, you think you've seen it all. Always go into the fact-find with an open mind. There's an old martial arts tale about a student who searches out the master of a different style to learn from him. The two meet and sit down for tea. Every time the old master says something, the hopeful disciple interrupts and says, "My style does that too." After about the fourth interruption, the frustrated master asks the would-be disciple if he'd like some more tea. The wise old man begins pouring tea into his cup. The tea begins to rise quickly to the top of the cup. The master continues to pour. Soon it rushes over the sides, spilling onto the table and then onto the young disciple's lap. "Enough," the young disciple screams, "my cup is full!" The wise old master calmly states, "Before you can learn, you must empty your cup." Never go into the fact-find with preconceived notions. Always empty your cup.

The next key to drilling down is continuing to dig until you strike oil. This is the hardest part of the fact-find. Too many times, sales associates ask great questions, they just don't ask enough about the same problem. In our example earlier, Dan got the answer he wanted. Todd told him he needed three big windows for the waiting room. Dan could have then taken the conversation to how many other windows or doors, but he decided to dig a little deeper. What were his findings? He was worried about the amount of heat those big windows would generate inside the waiting room. He was afraid his energy bills would be extremely high. He was afraid customers would be uncomfortable. (This was one of his main reasons for building in the first place.) Dan kept drilling until he struck oil. Dan's not out of the woods yet; they haven't even talked about the other windows or the garage doors, but he's already loaded his first bullet in his sales gun. Never go to the next question too early. Let the customer lead you to their itch (problem). If you can cultivate this skill, they will call you "Calamine lotion."

Lesson 15

Selling is Spelled C-O-N-S-U-L-T-I-N-G

In order to make the transition into soft selling, you must change your mindset. Look at a calendar. What day is it? From this day forward, you are no longer a salesperson; you, my friend, are a consultant. That wasn't hard at all, was it? Well, to be honest, there is a little more to it than that. Making the transition from sales to consultation isn't that difficult. "How do you do it?" you might be asking yourself. To start with, you need to understand the core differences between selling and consulting.

Salespeople have something tangible to sell. Consultants give advice. When salespeople see customers, their objective is to get the customer to spend their coins. When consultants see customers, they advise customers based on their needs, wants, desires, and pocketbooks. The sales associate tends to be aggressive in trying to close the sale. The consultant, on the other hand, just makes recommendations.

Think of it like a game of tug of war. The salesperson is on one side of the creek and the customer is on the other. The salesperson is pulling and yanking, trying to pull that customer into the creek (or pull them into signing a contract). The customer is on the other side, digging their feet into the muddy bank, making sure they don't buy something they don't want.

On the other hand, consultants are standing right beside the customer, helping them pull. The customer thinks of the consultant as their equal or ally because the consultant is looking out for their best interests.

Salespeople want the customer to buy a certain product or service. Consultants don't care. Listen to me closely here. I know that if the customer doesn't buy your products or services, you won't be in this occupation very long. However, I am saying you must solve the customer's problem. When I was working at the big Fortune 50, corporate decided that none of their direct sales force was to sell a certain smaller phone system. No, they weren't going to quit making the system, because there was a huge market for the product, and it had a very large customer base. The corporate *geniuses* were going to give the small phone systems to the dealer channel to sell, while we—the direct channel—were to sell customers on the bigger, more robust telephone system. The bigger system also had a bigger price, too. In fact, the bigger system's price point was usually 50-60 percent more than the small system's. If you added voicemail, the price was double. Since most of us were making our living on the small system, this came as quite a shock. In fact, during one of our sales meetings, one of my associates asked our manager, "Of our total sales in Kentucky, what percentage of revenue did the small systems account for?" My sales manager pulled out a sheet of paper to look at the numbers. Without making eye contact with any of us, he said, "Ninety percent." We had just been informed that the product that accounted for nearly all our revenue was not to be sold by us anymore.

Do you see why I left corporate America? Corporate had decided that we were to push this other product. There was no consideration given to our market or our customer base. They figured if we would just change our focus and push the bigger product, we would sell just as many as the small ones. In all their thinking, they forgot two important elements. First, not every customer needed, wanted, or desired all the bells and whistles of the bigger system. Second, just because I walked into the customer's office and said, "Hi, I'm Kent. I work for this big conglomerate," did not mean that the customer roll over and pay an extra fifty percent.

Consultation selling doesn't work that way. You don't make the customer fit the product or service, you make the product or service fit the individual customer. Let me warn you, if you're consultation selling, you will not sell every customer. The good thing is, as you will read in Lesson 19, you do not want every customer. Right now, though, let's move on to difference number three.

Salespeople need to sell products. Consultants solve problems. If you want to move from the stereotypical sales type into the profession of consulting, you've got to solve the customer's problems. Most aggressive salespeople walk into the customer's door with a fixed idea of what the customer needs.

The consultant, on the other hand, wants to find out what is making the customer itch, and scratch it. The best part of this scenario is, you scratch the itch with your products.

Salespeople worry about what their products and services cost. Consultants don't care about price. When I worked for the "man," some members of our team worried way too much about the cost of our products. Many times they worried so much, that they would go into their first "pitch" (not a consulting term, but one you will understand) with a twenty percent discount. If the customer wanted to negotiate, and most of them did, our sales associates would end up giving them even more. By the time the customer signed the contract, they had usually bought our products at a thirty to thirty-five percent off. It's no wonder they wanted us to quit selling the smaller system, we weren't selling anything; we were giving it away. In fact, one of my associates said we lose $10,000.00 on every sale, but we make it up with volume.

Here's a piece of advice: Don't spend the customer's money. The customer decides what is valuable to them and what isn't. Your job is to solve the problem. If your solution is twice the cost, but it does solve the dilemma, present it. Let the customer decide.

It's time for another war story. One time, Guy and I had an appointment at a small auto parts store. It was the best one-visit sale I had ever seen. Guy found out that this customer had a hard time getting all his calls because he was tying up all the outside lines. When our customer's business received a call for a certain part, his employees would put the call on hold, walk back through the shelves, find the part, return back to the counter, take the call off hold, and then tell the customer if the part was in stock. Our client had two problems. First, his customers were complaining of busy signals. The customer's outside lines were being tied up because of inefficient business practices. It was taking the counter help too long to see if the part was in stock. Guy and I had a great idea: Go wireless. However, there was a problem with our solution. We had a wireless headset that could answer one call at a time. It retailed for about $400.00. We also had a wireless telephone that could do everything an office phone could do. It could answer up to ten outside lines. It could conference call. You could program features on it. It had a huge amount of range. It also had a huge price, $1,200.00. Guy made the proposal with the more expensive phone because it was what would truly help the customer's business. They not only bought a new telephone system, but they bought two of the $1,200.00 telephones. It changed the way the customer did business. Guy consulted the customer. He let the customer decide if this solution was right for his business. Again, consultants never spend the customer's money.

Salespeople try to close the sale. Consultants do not. Let me ask you something. When you're out in the world, playing the role of consumer, do you like to be closed? When you're looking at that new car and the salesperson walks up and asks if you all can do business today, does that make you more or less likely to buy? When the Fortune 50 sent me to my initial sales training, we were taught to always ask for the business. In essence, we should always be looking to close the sale. I have yet to find a place in consultative selling for closing the customer. Consultation selling means you present the customer with the proper solution and let the customer decide. If you've done a proper job of discovering their itch and scratching it, the customer won't buy from anyone else but you.

Salespeople talk disparagingly about their competitors. Consultants do not (well maybe just a little). There are subtle ways

to talk badly about your competition without sounding bad. For example: "Our phone system uses modular plugs, so making additions, moves, and changes to your office can be as simple as plugging and unplugging. Their system is hardwired. That means if you need to make additions, moves, or changes, you've got to call their sorry service department and have one of their lazy, overpriced technicians come out and do it for you. That is, if you can get through to their service department." The competition got hit with so many derogatory comments, you almost feel obligated to buy it because it has such a bad reputation.

See how this sounds instead. "Ms. Customer, whether you buy from me or somebody else, make sure it's easy to make adds, moves, or changes. Since technician time usually costs about $150 an hour plus a premise visit, you'll want to be able to control some things yourself. I think one of the best things about our product is that it's easy to add phones or change things around in your office because you can plug and unplug the telephones yourself. Some of our competitors still require you to call a technician every time you want to make an add, move, or change." There, wasn't that more palatable? You sounded like a consultant. You can also bet that your customer will be asking the your competitor if their system uses modular plugs. Ouch. You also bought yourself some credibility because you told them ways they could save money by doing simple things themselves.

The biggest way to drive a consultation sale is to present what is best for the customer. In a later chapter, we'll talk about walking away. Remember, consultants are always on the customer's side.

Lesson 16

Blabidus
(Pronounced blab-eye-dus)

Do you talk a lot? Of course you do. You're in sales, right?
That's your job. You've got the "gift of gab." Customers see you
because you have the answers they want. You're paid to espouse
wisdom about a product or service. Let me ask you, if talking is so
important, why did God give you two ears and one mouth? In fact,
the Bible itself says, "My dear brothers, take note of this: Everyone
should be quick to listen, slow to speak…" (James 1:19).

Back in 1960, a song by Joe Jones went all the way to number
three on the pop charts. The title was "You Talk Too Much." The
song starts out (feel free to hum along if you know the melody),

"You talk too much, you worry me to death."

"You talk too much, you even worry my pet."

"You just taaaaaaaaaaaalk, talk too much."

This is one of the biggest problems salespeople have when they
get in front of the customer. They don't know when to shut up. There
are many reasons for this condition called "Blabidus" (pronounced

blab-eye-dus). Although I made this medical term up, it really is a disease that has killed many a good sale.

One of the reasons most salespeople blab so much is because we tend to be type-A personalities. We're usually very outgoing, somewhat brash. We tend to love to be the center of attention. In fact, it's my opinion that we begin choosing a career in sales very early. When I was in first grade, my report card was usually S (satisfactory) or S+; I even had the occasional E (excellent). However, the teacher's comments usually contained something like this, "Kent is a very likable student. However, he talks too much during class." Even at age six, I was trying to sell something.

The second symptom of Blabidus is trying to show the customer how smart you are. Let's be honest here. How many times have you caught yourself interrupting the customer when they're trying to tell you something? In fact, I'll bet there are times when you couldn't concentrate on what the customer saying because you were too busy thinking about that next killer feature your product had so you could *tell* them about it.

Here's the problem with Blabidus. It causes you to work too hard. The customer was willing to talk to you about their problem. In fact, I've had several customers know exactly what they want,  and basically sold themselves, all because I knew when to keep quiet. Silence is uncomfortable for people. Next time you're on a sales call, ask your open-ended question (we dealt with that earlier) and then shut up. Don't say another word. Look the customer deep in the eye and truly listen to what they say. You'll be amazed at how much relevant information they give. Don't ask another question immediately after they finish their sentence. Sit there. Many times, the customer will begin telling you something else you can use to sell your product or service.

Listening is not a natural skill. However, it can be learned. The best salespeople tend to be the best listeners. They're basically playing detective, looking for clues that help them sell more product. Proverbs 1:5 says it best: "Let the wise listen and add to their learning."

Lesson 17

You Are the Expert

We truly live in a fabulous time. In no other time in history has so much information been available to so many people. Just a couple of centuries ago, only the wealthy or the ordained could read. People lived in villages all their lives without ever traveling two miles down the road to the next village. Strangers in a town were an oddity.

Look at us today. We can get on plane and be anywhere in the world within a few hours. Who would have thought that there would ever come a time when you would need a twenty-four-hour news channel? Now we have a plethora of them to choose from. People can get on their computer and within seconds have information on virtually any subject. Our thirst for information is unquenchable.

However, our desire for knowledge can be a double-edged sword. In fact, many people only get half the information they need. You've no doubt heard someone say, "I know just enough about that to be dangerous." Chances are, they're right too. People pick up a computer magazine, read a few buzzwords, and suddenly they know about computers.

This chapter will discuss how you, the expert, can deal with the customer who thinks they know your business. Does this sound familiar? You've gone in to do a fact-find with a customer. You get all the information together for your proposal. You take the proposal back to the customer to get the deal worked. You walk into their office, where another person is there with your customer.

"Kent, I'd like you to meet my friend Bernice. I asked her to sit in with us today because her great uncle had a friend who worked for the telephone company back in 1962. She knows a little something about telephones."

Like what? She knows that if she hears a ringing sound coming from that magical box on her desk with the dangly cord, she can pick it up and say hello. Now I may be exaggerating a little bit, but you get the point. If Bernice knows so much about what I do, they why isn't she doing it? Maybe it's because she's inherently wealthy and she just wants to work at a dump like this to help keep her conscience clear. Is that it? Now that I've got that off my chest, let's deal with the "not-so-expert expert."

In today's world of information overload, you need to be prepared for the "expert" who really is not. The problem is, your customer is looking to them to sort out whether you're telling the truth or not. It's at this point that you have two options. Option A, talk over their head so high that they won't know what you're saying, making them feel stupid in the process. Option B, get them over to your side and have them sell the customer for you. Because I enjoy making money, I'll always choose B.

Here are a couple of war stories, one a success, one a miserable failure. Let's start with the bad and work our way to the good.

One time, I went out on a customer visit to do a fact-find for a telephone system. The customer knew someone who installed computer systems on the side. If you think that sounds fraught with peril, read on. Anyway, this computer expert had told his client that they needed to look at a telephone system that was compatible with high-speed digital telephone lines. This would not only allow them to use the digital lines for their voice calls, but it would also give them a much higher speed for their Internet access. He told the customer to give us the information and that he would be back to hold their hand when we made the proposal. The customer's needs weren't that complicated. However, the last thing the customer said was, "Our computer guy said that the phone system should be able to integrate with high-speed Internet access."

"What kind of high-speed Internet access do you plan on using?" I asked.

"We don't know. Our computer guy just said it should be compatible." (As you can imagine, that really narrowed everything down.)

"What are you going to do with high-speed Internet access?"

"Upload files like we're doing now."

"How do you do it now?"

"We use a dial-up modem."

"How's that working for you?"

"It works just fine, but he says we may want to go to high-speed in the future."

"Did he say when you all would be making the change?"

"He wasn't sure. It may be awhile, though."

"Well, is money going to be an issue?"

"Most definitely. Our old system is costing us business. We need a new phone system now."

"I'll work you up a couple of options. However, I'll probably need to talk to your computer guy. Can I have his number?"

"Sure, it's….."

Armed with all the information the customer could give me, I tried to get in touch with the computer guy. I left messages but the *expert* was too busy with his day job to return our calls. With no information, I did the proposal knowing I would probably have to make some adjustments once I met with the expert.

I talked to my friend, Guy, and he helped me get the proposal ready. I asked Guy if he would be willing to go to the customer meeting with me. I was afraid the computer guru would ask me a bunch of questions and I did not want to look stupid in front of the customer.

The day finally came and we went back to make our pitch. The expert was there. We asked some questions about what his plans were for their communications. Basically, the expert was building them a space shuttle, when all they needed was a go-cart.

We gave them a couple of options. Option 1 was what we thought would be best for the customer and their telephone needs. This option was based on all the information the customer had given us about what features and functionality they wanted from their phones. Option 2 was based on the expert's gaze into the future. As you can imagine, option 2 had a substantially higher price. During the meeting, we would ask the computer guy technical questions about why he wanted this or that. He didn't know. We would then hammer him, albeit in a nice way. In fact, we knew more about computers than he did. The problem was, we made him feel too insecure and he began to get defensive. We lost the deal because after we left, he said some unflattering things about us to the person who was writing the check. We were too smart for our own good. Be the expert, but allow the pseudo-expert to save face. Success in soft selling isn't judged by who is right. It is judged by who makes the most money. Like Teddy Roosevelt said, "Speak softly and carry a big stick." The problem was, we used our big stick to bash the guy's ego.

My second war story comes from one of my customers who owns a funeral home. This guy had an older model of the equipment I sell. He talked real fast. In fact, when he pulled up for our appointment, he almost ran through his own funeral home in his big SUV. Anyway, the technician and I walked in and he started talking. He said he knew a lot about our telephone systems. In fact, he had installed the one he at his business. He was having some problems and needed to know what could be done about it. I told him his processor was a little outdated and that it was probably time to look at replacing it. He asked me some questions and then said, "What's your best deal if I write you a check right now?"

"$1,500.00."

"Who do I make this out to?" he asked as he began writing me the check.

I wish those types of sales happened more often. After handing me the check, he said he had a friend who owned farm supply store. In fact, our man at the funeral home had installed the farm supply phone system as well. He told me to go see the guy. We hopped in the truck and headed for the farm supply store. This place needed a new processor as well. After talking to the owner for a while and figuring out his problems, I quoted him a price for the equipment he needed.

"I'll need to talk to my friend [the expert] and make sure this is what I need."

"Sure. Talk to him. If he feels like this is what you should do, just give me a call." Now I could have pushed a little, but I didn't have to. I knew the funeral home guy was going to sell this for me for two reasons. First, I gave him a good deal. Second, I let him be the expert. I was just the distribution warehouse.

The next day, the expert called me back. He said to order the equipment for the farm supply store. He basically sold me another $1,500.00 worth of equipment. Plus, the expert and I have become good friends and he has sold a couple of other systems for me since then.

The easiest way to be the expert is to be confident enough in your knowledge and abilities about what you do. Too often, salespeople want to *show* their knowledge as opposed to *sell* a product or service. I'm not saying if someone is way off base, that they shouldn't be corrected. I am saying, though, you've got to let people know you're the expert without being cocky and condescending. Be knowledgeable, be confident, and be comfortable. Remember, you are the expert.

Lesson 18

No Pressure

Let's pretend for a moment, shall we? You've just walked into the big electronics store. In this gargantuan warehouse with its sterile white walls, thousands of televisions, stereos, computers, and compact discs are stacked to the roof. You casually stroll over to the 200-inch televisions. As your begin looking at those big behemoths, you think about how much better professional wrestling (that's wrastlin' to us Southerners) would be on one of those big screens.

"Sir, are you interested in buying a TV?" asks the young, energetic sales clerk.

"I'm just kind of looking right now," you reply, wishing desperately to be left alone so you can step back into your world of the big television.

"Well, what sort of television are you looking for?"

"I'm really just looking right now. If I need anything, I'll let you know," you say in a firm tone, never making eye contact.

"Well, if you need anything, my name is Mario. I'll be right over there."

As old Mario heads off toward the end of the aisle, you realize your day of casual shopping is now in jeopardy. Every time you turn around, Mario seems to be there. In fact, if you went to the restroom, Mario would probably be in the stall next to you. With a feeling of frustration, you leave the mega electronics store.

Here's a war story that happened to a friend of mine. One time "Tom" and his fiancée went shopping for furniture. Remember, this is eastern Kentucky. There's this big furniture store out in the middle of nowhere. To explain the scope of this place, there were several buildings (I think he said they were barns, but I can't remember) strung together, and each was full of furniture. Tom and his fiancée had heard about this place and they decided to go check it out. When they got there, they were greeted by a friendly woman who told them to have a look around. Tom and his fiancée had barely taken three steps inside before a sales associate appeared. Tom told the associate that they didn't know exactly what they were looking for but when they figured it out, they'd come find him. "That's fine, take all the time you want. I'll be here when you need me." However, the salesperson would not leave them alone. In fact, he shadowed the couple throughout the entire complex. When they would leave one building and head to another, there he was, smiling and being friendly. The couple became so annoyed that they left the place without spending a dime.

It was really too bad, too, because Tom said he saw some decent furniture there. In fact, the couple had driven a couple of hours out into the boondocks just to see what the place had, because they had heard so much about the store. They were even prepared to buy some furniture that day because Tom said he had a blank check with him.

The problem was obviously the salesperson. In fact, my friend told me he had even discouraged people from shopping there because of their high-pressure tactics.

I've heard salespeople say they were low-pressure. My friend, in soft selling, there is no pressure. I know what you're saying: "You don't understand; at some point, you've got to try and close the sale. You've got to ask for the business." I was at a training course one time where one of my peers even said, "Always be closing." Now I want to ask you, do you like to be closed? Think about it a minute. When was the last time you bought something where the sales pressure was high? I never do. I don't like to be closed, it puts me on the defensive.

Since this book will end up being blackballed by every sales manager in the country anyway, I might as well say this: NEVER ASK FOR THE BUSINESS. I stand by the techniques and skills I've outlined in the previous lessons of this book. If you have to ask for the business, then you did not do your job as a salesperson to begin with. If you drilled deep enough, if you asked the right questions, if you read the customer properly  and if you did consultative selling, you won't have to ask the customer for the business; the customer will be asking you where to sign. No-pressure selling is relationship selling.

You see, most people don't like hard sales tactics. That's why car dealers have such a bad reputation. One day however, someone at General Motors came up with a novel idea. They decided to build a nameplate called a Saturn. The business model would be low-pressure selling. The price would be clearly marked, with no negotiation. To many people, this was a great way to do business. No longer would you make a clandestine visit to your local dealership under the cover of darkness at midnight. Now you could actually walk on the lot during the day, without having to talk to anyone if you didn't want to. You're probably saying that the Saturn nameplate may have stumbled a bit over the years, and you may be right. However, it brought a revolutionary way of doing business to the local new car dealership. In fact, many car dealers now incorporate no-pressure selling and no negotiations into their advertising.

One time, I was trying to sell a customer a telephone system. In fact, I had done a very good job of consultative selling and we had developed a very good client-customer relationship. Without any prodding from me, she was ready to sign a contract. After the papers were signed, I made the comment that I hadn't sold her the telephone system correctly.

"What do you mean?" she asked.

"According to all the sales training I've had, I did not sell you your telephone system properly. Our training always said to ask for the business. So I'm supposed to ask you, 'What will it take for us to do business today?' Instead, though, I just made the proposal and said 'If you have any questions, call me.'"

"Well, you may not have followed the procedures of your training, but if you had asked, 'What would it take for us to do business today?' I wouldn't have bought from you. Some salespeople don't understand that this is not a big city (although I don't think people in major metropolitan areas like high pressure either). That's not how I like to do business."

It's been my experience that people don't like pressure. They don't like to be closed. If you want to move into soft selling, you need to turn the pressure off. Now I know what you're saying, "What am I supposed do if a customer doesn't make an immediate decision? I mean, how can I contact a potential customer who has one of my proposals without appearing pushy or hard-selling?" A very good question, I must say. Turn the page and find out.

Lesson 19

All's Quiet on the Selling Front

Okay. You've got dozens of proposals out on the table, but nobody seems to be making a decision. In fact, there are some that seemed to be red hot two weeks ago, that if you said those same proposals were tepid today, you would be considered for an "Optimist of the Year" Award. So how do you contact customers who haven't made a decision to find out where they are in the buying process without appearing hard-sell and aggressive? There are several things you can do to find out where you stand, but let me tell you up front, you will rarely be able to push the buying decision along. That being said, read on.

One technique that I like to use is called the old "call 'em and ask 'em where we stand" (yes, this manuscript is very technical). It's a little blunt but it lets you know right away where the customer is in the buying decision. It goes something like this:

"Widget Works, to whom may I direct your call?"

"Mary, please."

"May I tell her who's calling?"

"Yes, this is Kent, the phone guy."

"One moment please."

"Hey Kent, how are you?"

"Not too good, Mary. In my business, no news usually isn't good news [this line is usually good for a laugh while still letting the customer know where you stand], so I just wanted to call and see if we were still in the game."

With that, Mary can tell me straight up if we've lost. If we have, I sometimes ask what made us lose. Was it price? Was it features? Usually the customer will be glad to tell you why they didn't buy your product or service. However, I did have a customer get very defensive about it one time. I guess she regretted her decision. I always like to know so I'll be better prepared the next time I go up against the same competitor. Now, some schools of thought say that you should try to get as much information as you can from them, because what have you got to lose? They didn't buy from you to begin with. Who cares if they get mad? I personally don't like to do that to the customer. This is where knowing your audience and reading them comes in. If I think they're embarrassed (and some of them are) I just say thanks for the opportunity and if they ever need anything, please don't hesitate to give me a call. You see, I want the customer to see nothing but professionalism. In fact, I want them to always have in the back of their mind that they made the wrong decision (so much for turning the other cheek). That way, when my competitor lets them down, I'll be there to catch them on the rebound.

If no decision has been made, you can take this opportunity to ask the customer if they have any questions about your proposal. Don't take up too much of the customer's time, otherwise the customer will feel pressure, even if it is unintentional.

This next technique has an innovative new name. It's called "shooting the bull." (I hope you realize I'm being sarcastic.) Shooting the bull is where you basically call the customer and say, "I was just looking through my day planner and saw your name. I just called to see how things were going." Sometimes the customer will tell you what's going on with your proposal. Sometimes they will just shoot the bull; hey, it's a shot. As a sidebar here, shooting the bull is a great way to keep up with your embedded base customers. Many times, your call will remind them that they needed to order something but they had not gotten around to calling you yet.

If you like the personal touch, you can try the "drop-in." You basically drop by the customer's site the next time you're in the area just to say hello. The drop-in has been very successful for me personally. However, a word of caution about the drop-in. First, you need to know the customer extremely well. If they consider you a pesky salesman to begin with, the drop-in will only reinforce that stereotype with the customer. Second, you need to be able to read the customer extremely well. If the customer appears frazzled or anxious, make your visit short and sweet. The longer you hang around, the more your personal stock in the customer's eyes will drop. The drop-in tends to work better on the "Mom and Pop" level than it does at the corporate level. At the corporate level, things tend to be more formal. Your contacts will have more meetings, and things tend to be on tighter schedules. The "Mom and Pop" level tends to hang a little looser.

The last technique for finding out where your customer is in their buying decision is a little more aggressive. In fact, when you use this technique, you're trying to push the buying decision along. I call it "upping the ante." In upping the ante, you are laying your cards out on the table. Be warned, upping the ante can take you completely out of the game, or it can cost you margin. However, it can motivate the customer to make a decision. In fact, department stores do it all the time. It's called the "sale."

"Widget Works, to whom may I direct your call?"

"Mary, please."

"May I tell her who's calling?"

"Yes, this is Kent, the phone guy."

"One moment please."

"Hey Kent, how are you?"

"Pretty good, Mary. I just wanted you to know that the price of those phones in my proposal has dropped significantly. They were going to cost you three hundred fifty bucks apiece, but I just received word that the company was needing to close a lot of business this month, so they dropped the price of each phone by fifty dollars. The price on those phones will be going back up on_____**[some specific date]**. I'm not trying to rush you. I just knew you were looking at that type of phone, so I wanted you to know."

Some rules apply for upping the ante. You must give the customer a specific time in which to act. Do not leave it in limbo. Otherwise, the customer will continue to sit on the decision, and then, if they buy a year later from you, they will expect the same price break. Don't tell the customer they need to decide today. Remember, you're a consultant. You're trying to do what's best for them. You've consulted this long; don't start acting like a slick-talking salesperson now.

I have found that upping the ante works extremely well in letter form. I don't know if money looks better in print form or what. (I do know that the newspaper carries an awful lot of sale ads.) I used a letter almost exactly like this one to nudge a sale along with a construction company that built retail office space.

Dear _____,

I know we haven't spoken in a while about your telephone needs, so that's why I am writing. I need a customer in the construction business that can be a good reference customer for me. If you will allow me to use you as a reference customer (provided you get the good service I know you expect), I will give you an additional 10 percent off the cost of your phone system. That will drop the cost by almost $500.00. I have included your original proposal, with the new discount added. If you'd like to discuss this in further detail, give me a call at (800) 555-1212. Thanks for your time and I look forward to hearing from you.

Sincerely,

Kent Berryman
Sterling Communications

That letter worked like a champ. In fact, the customer called me that same week and we signed a contract.

The world of sales, as you already know, is very cyclical. Sometimes everything you touch turns to gold. Sometimes it just turns to dust. Even when all's quiet on the selling front, there are still some proactive approaches that you can take to find out where the customer is in their buying decision, as well as ways you can nudge the process along, without appearing pushy or pestering.

Lesson 20

Know When to Hold 'em, Know When to Fold 'em

Kenny Rogers took that one hook phrase from a song called "The Gambler" and parlayed it into a number-one country hit. Plus, he made several made for TV movies about being "The Gambler." Here's to you, Kenny; truer words were never spoken.

I don't know if it's our competitive nature, a love of money, the thrill of the chase or what, but we salespeople hate to lose. To me, the only thing worse than losing the sale is the "no decision." You know the customer, the one you've visited three times because they want to buy something, but they want to keep you hanging in limbo.

At least with a loss, you know the score. The no decision is like a tie. Who wants a tie ballgame? Definitely not me. I want to win or lose. I'm sure that's why I don't like certain sports. That's why sometimes you've just got to walk away from certain sales and certain customers. Customers can be choosy. Why can't we? Let me tell you something. You don't want every customer.

Let's go to the old war chest and pull out a couple of stories. The first one comes from a music store that had some ancient telephone equipment. The phones were so old that I think they had cranks on them and you had to get Sarah from Mayberry to connect the call for you. One day, I received a call from a telephone technician friend of mine. He had been out to the music store on a case of telephone trouble. The store had a telephone system that was almost thirty years old; needless to say, it was getting harder and harder to find parts to fix it. In addition to no repair parts, the people who knew how to work on it had retired ages ago. Anyway, my technician friend told the owner that it might be time to look at replacing the system, because finding equipment and expertise to fix it was getting more difficult to do. The technician said he would have me give them a call. They agreed. I set up the appointment to see the owner. I arrived a couple of minutes early; my contact, I'll call her "Ms. X", wasn't there yet. A woman working in the store said she expected my contact to be there at any time. I said I was early, so I walked around the store.

Five minutes passed. No Ms. X. Ten minutes passed. No Ms. X. I continued to wait until half an hour had passed. I decided that if her phones were not important enough to give me the courtesy of a phone call to say she was going to be late, I was leaving this dump. As I walked out the front door, a big blue Lincoln Continental pulled up beside the building. As the woman was getting out, I walked over and introduced myself. Yes, she was Ms. X, the owner and my contact. We walked back into the store, where the other woman had been working. Ms. X introduced me to her daughter, the woman whom I had met earlier at the store. I still don't know why the daughter didn't tell me who she was. Ms. X said that her daughter could tell me everything about what they wanted in a phone system.

It's funny, the daughter knew I was the telephone man, yet she couldn't seem to tell me anything about the telephones for that half hour I was looking at old, dusty sheet music. I did, however, do a good fact-find. They wanted three desk telephones and would really like to have a wireless phone so a person could answer calls anywhere in the store. Also, the daughter felt like they needed an automated attendant so the caller could press one for her and two for her mother. Finally, for tax purposes, they said wanted to lease the telephone system. I told them I could have a proposal for them in a couple of days. So I set the follow-up appointment. On my way back to the office, my technician friend called me with some news.

"Kent, did you know that the music store has been renting those phones since 1972? They pay almost $100 per month to rent those. In fact, we added it up at the office. They've paid over $30,000 to rent those pieces of junk over the years."

My mouth hit the floorboard. Thirty thousand dollars to rent three telephones. This sale was in the bag. I knew that leasing the new equipment would be cheaper than what they were paying now. Plus, they wouldn't have trouble getting parts and service if they needed it.

When I got back to the office, I put their proposal together. New equipment. Wireless technology with greater flexibility. An automated attendant. All at $20.00 less per month than they were paying now.

I went back to the music store armed with brochures and a freshly printed contract. As usual, Ms. X was running a tad late; however, the daughter was glad to see me. I showed the daughter my brochures. She was truly impressed. I showed her my numbers. I showed her how she could have modern technology that could do countless more things at a price that was less than what her mother was paying now. She knew her mother would be ready to make a move. Their old phone system was giving them trouble and they knew it was about to die. Pop the top on the champagne, it's time to celebrate.

About that time, Ms. X came into the store. Her daughter was so excited, she did my presentation for me. This was great; the customer was selling themselves. I was just there, smiling and listening. I had taught the daughter well. The daughter handed it back to me for the leasing information.

"Yes Ms. X, the great thing about this is you can have new equipment, with a wireless phone and an auto attendant for about $20 less a month than you're currently paying now."

"Well, we'll think about it."

Uh-oh. We seemed to have a breakdown in communication. *"What's there to think about?"* I thought. Better equipment. Better customer service. Less money than you're already paying. This is a no-brainer. And then it hit me. This is the same customer who paid over $30,000 for three telephones.

"We'll probably do something in the next five years or so," Ms. X explained.

The daughter's shoulders began to droop as a look of fatigue came over her face. All the wind had been knocked out of her sails. Without saying a word, the daughter slowly walked back to her little metal desk at the other end of the store. I tried to get the look of confusion off my face, but I know I didn't hide it well.

I thanked Ms. X for her time and walked out of the store. As I was driving back to my office in a state of shock, it hit me: I didn't want Ms. X for a customer. Can you imagine trying to implement new technology to those people? You'd be getting ten or twelve calls a day, asking you stupid questions like, "What's a hold button do?" Stuff like that. The commission for selling them would not be worth the pain and aggravation they would cause.

I called my to tell him the whole ridiculous story. That's when Guy told me that he himself had tried to sell the same music store a couple of times with no success. Guess what? Every year or so, I get a call from a technician who says, "Hey, Kent, I just ran a case of trouble at a little music store. They have a really old phone switch, and I think you could sell them something new." About this time, I'll begin to laugh and tell the technician the whole story. And every year, this little music store pays another $1,200.00 for malfunctioning, outdated technology.

Sometimes, it truly is better to lose one. In fact, I can count five customers that I wish I had not shown up to sign the contract. You don't want every customer.

Here's war story number two. When I first started in the telephone business, I had an embedded base customer who had old equipment; in fact, it was the equipment exactly like the music store had. This company was owned by a man who was—let me say this in a nice way—not very pleasant to be around. The customer's business was a tree service; I'll call it "Little Saplings." This customer had been paying a monthly maintenance fee to us so we could keep his telephones working. The problem was, his phones were so out-of-date that the parts could not be found to keep them running. I guess I should have known that anyone who expects electronic technology to last that long probably still goes to a barber for all their dental care.

I had stopped by to see the man about a year earlier, but he did not show up for our appointment. I guess he was too busy doing community service. I left my business card with the receptionist. One day the following year, this man calls me up and leaves a message on my voice mail. Now remember, this guy has never met me before. He starts saying he's a working man and he knows how salespeople don't do anything all day, and that I was out on the golf course while he was trying to eke out a living in this cold, cruel world. My company was screwing him over because they were telling him parts could not be found to fix his thirty-year-old telephones. In between all this ranting and raving, he was cursing at me. Apparently, he'd never read Norman Vincent Peale's *How to Win Friends and Influence People*. I was over at Guy's house when I checked my messages. I proceeded to play the message to him.

"Let me give him a call," Guy said. "I've handled people like this before."

"No, I need to be the one to call this guy back," I retorted in a not-so-confident tone.

I called the Little Sapling's office and guess who answers? That's right, the irate customer himself.

"I know how you _____ salesmen are. Now I want my ___ _____ telephones fixed today. I'm getting tired of all this_____ from you people. I was getting ready to buy a new telephone system and I…"

97

I couldn't take any more as I interrupted him. "Now, wait just a minute. First, I don't let my friends curse me, much less people I've never met."

"Well, I…" the man stammered.

"Second, let me say that I don't want your business."

Silence filled the handset. I know he was expecting me to beg him to let me bid on his "new system," but it wasn't worth it. I mean, how could anyone be expected to please this guy?

"Who's your boss?"

"His name is Guy. Hold on a second and I'll let you talk to him." Guy really wasn't my supervisor, but he was as close as I could get at the time. I handed Guy the telephone.

"Yes sir, what can I do for you?"

"Your salesman just told me he didn't want my business."

"Yes I know, I heard him. If you have a problem with that, I'd be happy to come over to your office and discuss it with you."

The man stammered and stuttered a bit more and finally agreed to meet. Guy set up an appointment. Guess what? He didn't show up. Guy tried to reschedule the appointment but the man wouldn't return his calls.

You don't need or want every customer. I'm not telling you to be rude. What I am saying, though, is it's sometimes better to lose the sale than to lose your sanity. Sometimes, walking away is the best move you can make. Thanks, Kenny, you've given us all some great advice.

Lesson 21

Jambalaya

I started to call this chapter "Parting Shots," but it's almost dinnertime and I'm starting to get a little hungry. For those of you who don't know what jambalaya is, it's a Cajun dish that is made up of rice, beans, sausage, chicken, etc… It's a dish that is made up of ingredients someone has in their kitchen, but they don't have enough of one single thing to serve it by itself. That's what this chapter is. It's a chapter devoted to thoughts that I was unable to put anywhere else. So grab a fork and put on your bib, it's time for "Aaayeeee!," some good old jambalaya.

Cliches abound in our profession. One the most widely used ones when I worked at the Fortune 50 was "Plan your work, work your plan." Every year, my sales manager (who had never sold anything) would take all of the sales associates into his office for a sit-down meeting of how we were going to make our quotas over the next year. Each year, we would write down things like drive our territories more often to see what new buildings were going up so we could do more "smokestacking," make more cold calls (yea, right), call every customer we had once a year, and other things like that. The problem was, we would spend so much time planning that we didn't have time to do our jobs. In fact, I've seen many salespeople plan their way right out of a job. They could make fantastic spreadsheets. Track their time to the second each day. They just couldn't sell. To me, selling is a dynamic organism in motion. Each day can bring new challenges. Think about the last time you had your day all planned. Suddenly, a customer calls and needs a proposal today. So you start working on a proposal and "WHAMO," one of your major accounts is having a billing issue. Suddenly, your plans have been shattered like glass. What I'm trying to emphasize is, don't get so caught up in the planning that you lose sight of the goal. That goal, obviously, is selling.

Sometimes you've got to just play the game. If you are a sales associate for a big corporation, you know how much red tape there can be. This can become very frustrating because you represent the big corporation to the customer. The customer doesn't care that someone on a loading dock in Albuquerque didn't get their order on the truck. All that customer knows is you said it would be there yesterday and it didn't show up. You're to blame, even though it wasn't your fault. You're not going to believe this, but sometimes big corporations lose orders, miss deadlines, and bill customers wrong. You've basically got two options. Option one, you can leave. Option two, you can stay. If you the thought of leaving the world of good pay and benefits behind to start something for yourself seems a little risky, then you just have to play the game. Know going in that big companies make mistakes. You aren't going to change them. Remember Lesson 1: Cold calling has been an out-of-date selling model for over fifty years, yet it is still required by multi-billion-dollar corporations. Since they aren't going to change, you have to. When I say change, I don't mean your personality, I mean your expectations. Realize that mistakes are going to be made that are outside your personal control. Understand that there are always going to be protocols and procedures that are going to be a waste of time. If you're frustrated with all the problems that corporate America has, but you like having a regular paycheck, change your expectations. Otherwise, you'll be driven crazy by corporate incompetence.

Believe in what you sell. If I was going to give any new sales associate one piece of advice, this is it. If you've read this entire book, then you know that my first job out of college was selling cable television ads. In case you didn't get it the first time, I was pretty good at it. I was told that advertising on cable television was better than advertising with the local newspaper or on the local radio station because we had the advantage of moving pictures and sound. One day, I decided to sit down and run the numbers for myself. Uh-oh. Houston, we have a problem. After running the numbers, I found out that the service I was selling had a lot less reach. In other words, I had moving pictures and sound, but I didn't have a lot of viewers watching. A top-rated cable show in a town of 10,000 people might only have 200 viewers. Compared with the local newspaper that sold 5,000 copies, or the local radio station that reaches three counties, my product in my opinion, was the worst value. I lost all belief in what I sold. I said all that to say this: You've got to believe it if you're going to sell it. When you believe in what you sell, you have a certain enthusiasm that can't be hidden. Customers see it. It's something you can't fake.

Have fun and enjoy your work. In order to be successful in this world, you need to enjoy what you do. I have a friend named "Willy". Willy works for a large automobile manufacturer. Willy was a supervisor with a couple of different shifts under his control. Willy hated his job. He didn't get home until seven or eight o'clock at night. He got calls at all hours. His little girl was growing up and he wasn't there to see it. Willy was miserable. We would talk about it all the time. Willy called it the "golden handcuffs." He hated his job but his salary was too good. He was locked in. Willy applied for other jobs within the company but he never got them. Finally, a job opened up for the supervisor of the buildings and grounds crew. This job was right up his alley. Willy likes to tinker and build things around the house. I would call him a Mr. Fix-It. Even though it was considered a lateral move or as some said, "a step down," Willy applied. He was offered the job. Suddenly, doubt began to creep in. Willy wasn't sure whether he should take the job. Although he didn't like his current position, Willy was comfortable in it. He asked me about it.

"Man, I just don't know what to do."

"Do you think you'd like the job?"

"I'd love it."

"Would you be on call twenty-four hours a day like you are now?"

"There may be a time where I'd have to occasionally work late, but not to the degree that I'm working now."

"What does your wife say?"

"She thinks it would be the perfect job for me. Plus, I'd be getting home at a decent hour."

"How's the pay?"

"It may be a slight drop in pay, but there wouldn't be the stress."

"Does it matter that it may pay less?"

"Not really."

"Then why don't you take the job? It sounds to me like it's a gift from God."

"Well, I've had some people tell me that if I take this job, then I probably wouldn't be considered for future promotions to move up in the company."

"Do you really want to move up and have more stress?"

"No, not at all."

"Then it sounds to me like this is the job for you. Besides, who cares if you never get promoted again? You may not get promoted, staying in the position you are in now. You'll get to see your family more. You'll be doing a job you love. It sounds to me like you'd be crazy not to take the job."

Willy took the job. He tells me that it was the best career decision he's ever made. Enjoy what you do. You'll look forward to going to work.

Help new associates learn the ropes. I wouldn't be in the position I am in today if my friend Guy hadn't helped me learn the ropes. Now let me say this. Guy didn't do my work for me. In fact, sometimes it would have been easier on both of us if he had. Guy forced me to work hard to learn the telephone business. It was really frustrating for me because he would do other associates' jobs when they'd ask for help. Every time I had a problem, he would point me in the direction I needed to go. However, he wouldn't fix the problem for me. One day,

I asked him why he made me do all this work when he'd basically fix the other associates' problems. He reeled off an old proverb: "Give a man a fish and he eats today. Teach a man to fish and he eats for a lifetime." I know that in your busy schedule, you may think there isn't time to help the "new person" learn the ropes. I challenge you, though, if there is someone new in your organization struggling with the job, take them under your wing. Show them the ropes. Not only will this give you great satisfaction as they learn and grow, but it will also give you an ally and supporter if you ever need help.

Finally, sometimes you just have to take a day off. If you've been in sales for any length of time, there are days when everything you touch just disintegrates right before you eyes. It's those days that you just have to walk away for a while. Good salespeople know this. Walk away for a day or two. Relax. Play golf. Don't do anything work related. Don't even look at a trade publication. When you come back, you'll feel refreshed. When nothing's going right, take a day off.

www.ingramcontent.com/pod-product-compliance
Lightning Source LLC
Chambersburg PA
CBHW022019170526
45157CB00003B/1288